EDGE OF
THE EDGE

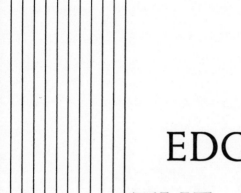

EDGE OF
THE EDGE

By Theodore E. Matson

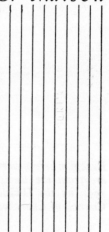

FRIENDSHIP
PRESS

NEW YORK

COPYRIGHT © 1961 BY FRIENDSHIP PRESS, INC.
LIBRARY OF CONGRESS NUMBER: 61–6627
PRINTED IN THE UNITED STATES OF AMERICA

1254936

CONTENTS

CONTENTS

FOREWORD

*T*he thesis of this book is that the church is in the midst of today's vast social upheaval but must not be caught in it. While the church operates within the time and space situation and neither despises nor detaches itself from the world drama, it lives in continual awareness that Christ's kingdom is not of this world. To make Christ the King known is the task to which the church has been called in the unfolding purposes of his kingdom.

Grateful acknowledgment is made to the Commission on Missionary Education and its editors for invaluable assistance at every stage of writing this book. I am especially appreciative of the encouragement and suggestions given me by my colleagues of the board and staff of the Division of Home Missions of the National Council of Churches. I am also grateful to the scores of men and women in churches in the United States and Canada with whom I have talked and whose insights are reflected in practically every chapter.

THEODORE E. MATSON

1:

THESE

TIMES

Man has always lived in change. But no generation before ours has seen changes on such a vast scale. They come in rapid, staccato fashion. Cataclysmic changes are taking place in the minds of men, in our family relationships, in the places where we work, in the nation and throughout the world.

"At some unmarked point during the last twenty years," observes Peter F. Drucker, educator, author, and management consultant, in the introduction of his *Landmarks of Tomorrow*, "we imperceptibly moved out of the modern age and into a new, as yet nameless era. . . . The old view of the world, the old task and the old center, calling themselves 'modern' and 'up to date' only a few years ago, just make no sense any more. . . . Our actions are already measured against the stern demands of the 'today,' the 'post-modern' world; and yet we have no theories, no concepts, no slogans—no real knowledge—about the new reality." [1]

The changes have been accomplished without violence and without much noticeable upset, but the tempo of change is revolutionary. Indeed, if people who lived in the nineteenth century could have foreseen what we see, they wouldn't have believed it.

Our minds do not really grasp what is happening. We only know we are living in a new America—new in everything from the transformed landscape outside the picture window to our changed attitudes toward work and pleasure.

The mood of America is to look for the new—in cars, rockets, satellites, suburban developments, personalities, scientists, and amusement.

Our belief in ongoing progress has made social institutions, traditionally set against change, open to change. We accept change as norm. The question whether it is for better or worse hardly rises. The counsel of St. Paul to "prove what is good" gets little hearing.

AGE OF PUSH BUTTONS

Walter Reuther, president of the CIO Division of the AFL-CIO, has expressed the opinion that the tremendous impact of the industrial revolution in the first half of the twentieth century will be topped by the technological revolution of the century's second fifty years.

In offices a whole array of ingenious new machines are in operation. Automatic "clerks"—electric computers, calculating machines, all sorts of devices to speed clerical tasks—are doing jobs that until recently demanded human effort. There are machines in process of development that will, among other things, forecast the weather, read printed instructions, act on spoken orders, translate printed English into Braille, and send data from coast to coast in an instant.

In the relatively near future a satellite with electronic

equipment will be able to flash programs onto our TV screens from any point on the globe. In less than five years, a navigator on a ship or plane will no longer need a sextant or a radio beam finder to get a "fix" on his position—he will tune in on a satellite four hundred miles overhead. Already dogs have been shot into space and serious talk about moon landings takes place outside the pages of science fiction magazines.

OUR SHRUNKEN WORLD

Radio, whose voices encircle the globe on electric waves, and television, which gives faces to voices, have made the world a neighborhood. All men are in communication for the first time in history. What happens on one side of the world is known on the other side in a matter of minutes. As for travel, a man living in New York is closer in time to London and Moscow than he was to Boston fifty years ago.

Dr. Walter R. Dornberger, guided missile consultant of the Bell Aircraft Corporation, believes that within twenty or thirty years we shall be able to reserve a seat on a Dyna-Soar-type passenger plane (aerospacecraft) that will take us virtually anyplace on the face of the globe in less than an hour and a quarter, or around the world in less than three hours. The new miracle plane is expected to be ready for test flying in 1967. It is unlikely, Dr. Dornberger says, that aerospacecraft will ever be used for such "short hauls" as a 2,800 mile coast-to-coast U.S. flight. Supersonic jet transports, flying at 2,000 to 2,500 miles per hour, should be satisfactory for domestic travel.

No matter where we live today the world is rushing in on us. More than a hundred thousand Americans live and work abroad—business men, consular officials, exchange students, scientists, missionaries, educators, interpreters. Tourists by the million cover practically every nook and cranny of the world, and a wit has given a new commandment, "Go into all the world and take pictures of all nations."

Tens of thousands of people from all parts of the world live and work in America. We used to think of neighbors as people of our own kind but ". . . now suddenly the foreigners have become neighbors and the neighbors have become foreigners." [2]

Affairs that only a few years ago were considered local now are recognized as having world-wide implications. This is especially true of racial conflicts and inequities.

The Monroe Doctrine as an isolation policy was against any entangling alliances and was completely in keeping with the traditional American approach to make and keep America the New World. This was to be "the land of the free and the home of the brave" and to that end isolation, it was believed, was of the essence.

Time has a way of changing the course of history. During this century we have been involved in two world wars. We are now active partners in the United Nations, and we have military bases in all parts of the world. Nationally and privately we have our vested interests in all parts of the world. The possibility of another war horrifies us because we know the unthinkable destruction such a war would bring.

We live in times when applied science has shortened miles and unified our shrinking world, but at the same time threatens mankind with annihilation. The earth has become one neighborhood before we have learned how to be neighbors.

URBAN POPULATION REVOLUTION

Urban growth is not a phenomenon peculiar to the United States. More than fifty years ago, H. G. Wells wrote of the modern great city as looking like something that had burst an intolerable envelope and splashed.

However, the rapid increase of the U.S. urban population in proportion to the total population is unprecedented. The *Architectural Forum* stated editorially in its September, 1959, issue: ". . . pushing with inexorable force, is an urban population revolution which, beginning about World War II, is just now approaching full tide. This is the phenomenon known as 'scatteration' or 'the exploding metropolis,' described by Coleman Woodbury, director of urban research at the University of Wisconsin, as a 'new pattern of settlement.' " [3] By 1975, the urban areas are expected to have 60 million more inhabitants than in 1950, or an increase of 71 per cent. In other words, the probable increase in metropolitan population by 1975, according to the Ford Foundation, will equal the combined populations of the metropolitan areas of New York, northeastern New Jersey, Chicago, Los Angeles, Philadelphia, Detroit, Boston, San Francisco, Oakland, Pittsburgh, St. Louis, Cleveland, Washington, Baltimore, Minneapolis, St. Paul, and Buffalo, plus 15 million more. There are seventeen definable urban regions today, dominated by central cities.

We are familiar with the metropolitan areas that stretch from Boston to Washington, D.C., and those that run from Milwaukee south and east to Chicago and South Bend, Ind., but in recent years even states such as Colorado, Utah, and Arizona have become metropolitan.

In 1910 three out of four Texans lived in rural communities. There was not a Texas city with as many as a hundred thousand inhabitants. Two out of three Texans now live in urban areas; 146 of the 254 counties of Texas have lost population since 1910. It is expected that by 1975 the city of Houston will have a population of more than 2,000,000; Dallas and San Antonio, 1,400,000; Fort Worth, 1,000,000.

By the year 2000 the city will dominate every section of the country, according to an extensive population study, "Metropolitanization of the United States," released late in 1959 by the Urban Land Institute of Washington, D.C. The study indicates that 85 per cent of the country's population at the end of the century, estimated at some 300 to 320 million, will live in urban areas.

President Eisenhower in his State of the Union Message to Congress in January, 1960, stated, "We are . . . witnessing explosive growth in metropolitan areas" and "The roster of urban problems . . . is staggering."

New York's Mayor Robert F. Wagner told the National Municipal League meeting in Springfield, Mass., in November, 1959, that the biggest challenge of the 1960's is to awaken fully to the fact that we are an urban nation.

The cities of America, with their dilemmas and the question of their future, must rank as the great unspoken, overlooked, underplayed problem of our time. The suburbs are part and parcel of pan-urbia. The rise of suburbia has been noted as one of the social revolutions of our day. At the same time, we know that suburbanization is simply the current thrust in the ongoing process by which all our metropolitan areas have grown from their inception. It is the push of people toward the metropolis that causes it to expand into the countryside. During the last three decades the suburban population increased 210 per cent while the nation as a whole increased only 64 per cent. Today suburbia is the home of some ". . . 60 million people who represent every patch of democracy's hand-stitched quilt, every economic layer, every laboring and professional pursuit in the country." [4]

All is not well with the suburbs. Sections of older ones have deteriorated badly. The housing in a great many of the new suburbs is so poor that they already have a slum-like appearance. Schools are understaffed and overcrowded. Transportation problems increase. Buses and suburban trains are overcrowded and often late. The highways are jammed, and the end of the jamming is nowhere in sight, since it is estimated that by 1975 there will be more than a hundred million cars on the streets, highways, and byways of the nation.

Beyond the suburbs are the exurbs. The population in many of the exurbs has become so dense that they have been classified as urban (formerly rural) in the 1960 United States census.

Urban growth has outrun political boundaries. In *The New York Times* Clayton Knowles wrote:

Wanted: tools of government to run atomic-age America. The machinery of yesterday is outmoded. Expanding urbanization and industrialization have created a challenging metropolitan problem. Old concepts of how to run a city, suburb, and even open country are shattered. In north, south, east, and west Americans grope for a way to deal effectively with basic considerations like health and housing, transportation and trade, because they spell boundaries of great cities.[5]

THE HOMOGENOUS LIFE

There is a growing tendency toward the homogenization of American culture, due primarily to the growth of the middle income class, which is putting the stamp of its tastes and interests on our entire society. White collar workers increased in numbers from 5,115,000 in 1900 to 21,600,000 in 1950; they constituted 36.6 per cent of the working population in 1950, compared to 17.6 in 1900. Between 1900 and 1956 the number of engineers, reports economist Sumner H. Slichter, increased from 41,000 to 850,000. The number of common laborers dropped from 8,900,000 to 5,900,000 during the same period of time, which means from one fourth of the employed to one eleventh.

The fact that national backgrounds today have less meaning adds to this homogenization. This de-emphasizing of nationality is understandable, since 85 per cent of the United States population are at least of the third generation of immigrant families.

Movies, radio, television, mass circulation magazines and newspapers are generally planned for all America, and thus they tend to homogenize culture largely according to the norms of the urban areas where they originate. One might say that ours is an homogenized, pan-urban culture.

There was a time when one could easily label a man a Republican or a Democrat. Today's candidates for office could switch from one party to another and feel very much at home. Only a few years ago it was unusual for a voter to cross party lines or "scratch" his ticket. Today it is common practice.

Whether we like it or not, religious differences are also

less meaningful. There is less concern about the content of religion. This is especially true in the suburbs. The emphasis today seems to be on "fellowship," "togetherness," "tolerance," "the golden rule," "religion in general." In fact, "Just as cultural values and symbols of national unity take on a generalized content, so also theological doctrines assume a diffused meaning, and become 'all things to all men' to which all may subscribe." [6]

RELIGION IN AMERICA

There is developing, or perhaps has already been developed, a wider, more intense, and more complete secularization of culture than the world has ever known. Christopher Dawson charges in *Religion and Culture:*

The new scientific culture is devoid of all positive spiritual content. It is an immense complex of technique and specialisms without a guiding spirit, with no common basis of common moral values, with no unifying spiritual aim.

. . . Indeed it may become the enemy of human life itself and the victory of technocracy may mean the destruction of humanity, since it is impossible to ignore the way in which the latest triumphs of applied science have been turned to destructive ends.[7]

According to Martin E. Marty in *The New Shape of American Religion*, America has moved into a post-Protestant era. While Protestantism retains its statistical plurality among the three traditional faiths, it is no longer the predominant force shaping the common life in the way that Protestant Puritanism and Protestant evangelization once determined the contours of American culture. At some critical points it has yielded influence to the other historic faiths. America has become urbanized; and with few exceptions outside the South, Catholicism controls urban centers. Further, "Because of Protestantism's divisions, unassertiveness, and lack of symbolism, Catholicism tends to dominate the mass media." [8] Meanwhile, Dr. Marty asserts, Jewish culture has assumed a dominant role in the world of entertainment and the arts.

Dr. Marty contends, with valid argument, that each wave of revivalism has brought with it the erosion of the particular, the smoothing of the edges of witness, the loss of religious content; and a religion-in-general is the religion in America today. The net result is that we have come up with a packaged god.

The god of America's religion-in-general is a god made in man's image. He is manageable; he is comforting (but his holiness is ignored); he is one of us, an American jolly good fellow. Popular song makes him "a livin' doll" or the "Man Upstairs." "Sometimes," comments Marty, "when instinct winces at such blasphemy, God is identified as someone in the great somewhere, or simply as 'He'." [9]

William Lee Miller, of Yale Divinity School, laments that the drive toward a shallow and *compulsory common creed* —a kind of religion-in-general, superficial and syncretistic— is destroying the profounder elements of faith.

There are more than a few who compare the church to an old man who has a long list of distinguished achievements and many merit awards but is no longer productive. They insist that the church today is not an effective force.

In any event, it is becoming more apparent with every passing day that the prevailing morality in the United States and Canada does not reflect the influence of the Christian message. In the most crucial issues of life—friendship and love, marriage and home, death and burial—members of the churches obey submissively the dictates of American culture and public opinion rather than the claims of the Christian gospel.

Trenchantly Lawrence D. Folkemer asserts:

Religiosity and secularism pace each other down the street. Never has there been a greater dichotomy of faith and life than in modern society. On the one hand, an insatiable religious appetite and on the other an uncontrollable propensity to worship at secular altars. Where men place their offerings and center their primary interests is where their real religion is to be found. Is God, God; or is he a god?" [10]

MAN'S DILEMMA

One observer calls attention to the "thingamization" of man. He is depersonalized by his lostness in the mass, by the manipulative technique, by being a tool of organization, by marketing programs that make him a thing. He both belongs and conforms.

There is an interesting line in Eugene O'Neill's fantastic play, *The Great God Brown*. When the central figure, Brown, lies dead on the street, a policeman bends over his body and asks, "Well, what's his name?" Someone replies, "Man." Then the policeman, pencil poised over notebook, asks "How do you spell it?"

The big things that affect the lives of people are decided elsewhere, often without consideration for the welfare of the people. Factories relocate and no questions are asked. By sheer force of economic circumstances people move in all directions. Tens of thousands move north from southern communities and are quite unprepared for the urban pattern of living. Northerners move South with industry and suddenly the South becomes a new South. But whether a man stays or moves he has become a thing.

Today men wonder if human personality has any value at all, since they are pushed about by impersonal forces on every side. This era of collectivism, technology, automation, and great scale industry prompts us to ask, rather fearfully, "How important is an individual as over against the mass achievements of our industrial age?" Man finds himself swimming with the tide and at the same time afraid that he will be drowned by the next wave that strikes him.

Margaret Meade tellingly points out the fact that we have become a generation of nest builders. We go in everywhere to squeeze out as much as we can and assume as little responsibility as possible. Aware of our insecurity, we nonetheless optimistically seek out such security as we can. Most of us have no real concern about such problems as juvenile delinquency, slum conditions, immoral literature, broken homes, and our fragmented church.

We are tired cogs in a fast moving machine. We argue politics and ride the bandwagon; yet we do not trust politicians. We zoom through space; yet we have trouble walking the earth with honor and hope. We talk confidently, but fear lurks within. We live on mortgages and temporize on eternity.

Our world is a tangle of shattered relationships. Homes are broken, agreements are scorned, the political merry-go-round is a mad scramble for party control and power, racial pride divides men, pressure of one kind or another squeezes men into a mold and nations look at one another with suspicion, hatred, or fear.

"We feel ourselves beleaguered by happenings" is the judgment of Robert L. Heilbroner, "which seem not only malign and intransigent, but unpredictable. . . . The future itself is a direction in which we look no longer with confidence but with vague forebodings and a sense of unpreparedness. . . . If the future seems to be a kind of limbo, a repository of endless surprises, it is because we no longer see it as the expected culmination of the past, as the growing edge of the present. . . . Unlike our forefathers who lived very much in history and for history, we ourselves appear to be adrift in an historic void." [11]

The June 10, 1959, *Saturday Evening Post* cover by artist Norman Rockwell pictures a capped and gowned college graduate, diploma in hand, standing alone against a background of news clippings that reveal the jeopardous character of the adult world he is about to enter. The young graduate wears a puzzled expression which seems to ask, "Where do I go from here?"

2:

THE UNCHANGING
AND THE UNFINISHED

We are in midstream today. If there is one thing we can expect, it is change. And many of the changes will come, as they have come, unannounced. It is a time when no one can take for granted the world he lives in, the things he holds dear, or the values and truths that to him seem constant. It is a time when we are compelled by events to stand off and take stock.

Many people are bewildered by the confusion and the complexities that surround them. On the one hand they feel hemmed in and on the other hand they have the sense of being pushed on by some inexorable force. They ask, "Is there no way out? Does life have no meaning, no purpose? Is there no positive word that speaks to our condition?"

It is certain that man does not have the answer. But God has given the answer. He has given the answer in Jesus Christ. In becoming man, living, suffering, dying, rising, ascending—God gave the answer to a world of confusion and broken relationships. In the words of J. B. Phillips, "The historic fact remains, and we in the twentieth century . . . may have to short-circuit the centuries and let the startling truth break over us afresh—that we live on a visited planet." [1]

We do not know what the future will bring—God keeps a veil over our tomorrows—and we need not be fretful about it. We do know that God has a plan and purpose for men and the world. We do know what God has done in history—that the death and resurrection of Jesus Christ makes all the difference.

A World Council of Churches report said:

That mighty event is faith's assurance that Christ has overcome the world and all the powers of evil, sin, and death; it is the beginning of a new life in the power of the Spirit; it is the guarantee of God's promise that in His good time His victory will be manifest to all, His Kingdom come in glory, and He Himself be known everywhere as King. It therefore begets a living hope. . . . Our hope comes to us from God and rests in God. [2]

In this glad faith and confidence we can carry on our work without panic or fear even though we know that we live under the threat of atomic annihilation. We can witness to the love of God and his power to save sinners—which we know through our experiences. We can work relentlessly toward racial, economic, social, and personal reconciliation, since the floor is level at the foot of the Cross —all barriers are broken down. Each one of us can and must do what he is able to relieve the world's pain and tragedy. It was the Resurrection faith that lighted up the first century world and that today can illuminate a planet threatened by the darkness of wholesale destruction.

We need not be overoccupied with the world's demands,

deluded by its dazzlements, nor hemmed in by its limitations.

We go into a world where Jesus Christ is Savior and Lord, in order that the news of his Kingship may be proclaimed, "That through the church the manifold wisdom of God might now be made known." [3]

THE WORD FROM THE BEYOND

The church proclaims the good news not only as the answer to a man's dilemma, but as the answer in every age and every place. It dares to state that only in terms of the Cross and Resurrection of Jesus Christ are men and women able to come to grips with life's reality, with life's changes, and with life's finality without surrender or self deception or despair. The Cross is not in the sky. It is planted on the earth, wherefore ". . . he is able for all time to save those who draw near to God through him, since he always lives to make intercession for them." [4]

When as Christians we say, "I believe in God," we mean, "I believe that this is a real world and here I am committed to live a real life. I believe it is God's world and that it is coming out somewhere. I believe this world has a spiritual purpose, and that this purpose is made manifest in the life of Jesus Christ, in his death and Resurrection—that he is the hope of the world. I believe, therefore, that in him I and all men may live creatively and victoriously, come what may."

We have the "word from the beyond" for man's predicament, mediated through history and alive and creative through the Holy Spirit in the life of the Body of Christ, the Church. In that confidence, St. Paul could say, "I know whom I have believed," [5] and ". . . we are more than conquerors through him who loved us. For I am sure that neither death, nor life . . . nor things present, nor things to come . . . will be able to separate us from the love of God in Christ Jesus our Lord." [6]

Until the end of time Christ continues to act through the ongoing life of that Body that he claims as his own. And in his own time—the right time—he will bring his work of creation and redemption to fulfillment. Until that time comes the Church, his Body, is on mission sent.

ON MISSION SENT

When Jesus said to his disciples, "As the Father has sent me, even so I send you," [7] he was committing them to that mission that he had himself carried as the sent one of his Father and which the church was now to carry to all men. The church lives in history as a witness to his lordship. "You shall be my witnesses." [8]

The territory assigned to the church includes the whole world. "Go therefore and make disciples of all nations." [9] This territory has already been claimed by our Lord. The specific task of the church is to proclaim the kingship of its Lord and to hasten the day of his coming in glory by its missionary activity.

The world to which we address the gospel is therefore not an alien world to be renounced but a world that has been redeemed. "God was in Christ reconciling the world to himself, not counting their trespasses against them." [10]

In the commission to go and make disciples, we hear the unchanging charter of the unchanging mission of the church in history. It cannot be suspended because of rapid social changes or changing historical circumstances or because no road map has been provided. There is, however, a sure promise that accompanies the commission, ". . . lo, I am with you always, to the close of the age." [11] He is in his church and with his church forever.

Come what may, the church's mission remains unchanging and ongoing because the purposes of God do not change. Come what may we ". . . run with perseverance the race that is set before us, looking to Jesus the pioneer and perfecter of our faith" [12] because the future is God's.

What is behind is done. We could not change it if we wanted to. If we are wise we will learn from it. What is ahead we do not know, but the future is always more significant for the unfinished plan of God than the past.

There are those who have asked, "Why does the Acts of the Apostles end with Paul in prison awaiting judgment?" We like success stories. No doubt St. Luke ends the story in the way he does because Paul's work was finished. He had shown how the faith began in Jerusalem and swept across the world until it reached the great city of Rome. He ended where the apostles were to leave off, since it is a continuing story. Each generation writes a chapter in the church's history and until the end of the dispensation of grace each chapter can and must read, "To be continued."

All the generations of all the people of all the lands of all the world are dependent on whether or not we Christians today tell the story of God's wonderful deed in Jesus Christ. This is essentially the church's task and it is clearly the primary task of all of us. Today we are the ones who have heard the story and say we believe it. That which distinguishes us as Christians is not that we have been reconciled to God. All the world has been reconciled. That which dis-

tinguishes us is that we are now the ones who have accepted
the gift of God's reconciliation and to us has been entrusted
the message of reconciliation. "So we are ambassadors for
Christ, God making his appeal through us. We beseech you
on behalf of Christ, be reconciled to God." [13] We who
are heirs of salvation, by the grace and mercy of God, have
the commission to tell others that they, too, share in the inheritance. Reuel L. Howe says:

If there is anything that we are doing as individuals or as parishes that does not fit into this reconciling purpose, then it is
not our business; and if there is anything we ought to be doing
that fits into it, then we must make it our business. . . . Reconciliation is one of the key words for understanding the purpose
of the Christian ministry, which belongs as much to the laity as
to the clergy.[14]

It is clear that we are to carry the message to the whole
world, because it is the whole world that God has reconciled
to himself. There is no man too far away to receive the
good news. By the same token, there is no one too near to
receive the good news. If we do not recognize this we shall
think of our missionary enterprise as giving something to
some people that does not already belong to them. Our
task is to make sure that all men are aware of their inheritance in Jesus Christ. Whether they accept this inheritance
is beside the point.

Horace Crotty pointed out in *The Church Victorious:*

Christ knew what He was saying when He told us to go out
into 'all the world.' He knew that we must win over the whole
field and front of life, or not at all. You cannot evangelize bits

of men, bits of his personality, bits of his society, or his world.
Christian victory . . . is indivisible. This is the real meaning of
the missionary enterprise and call. It embraces so much more
than what we commonly and wrongfully describe as 'foreign'
missions, for indeed there are no foreigners in the great family
of Christ.[15]

"It would be a healthy thing," says Charles W. Forman
in *A Faith for the Nations* "if there were a church courageous enough to refuse to accept money for support of
foreign missions from people who failed to do anything
about the mission right outside their doorstep, and which
refused to let people preach to the local community who
were not also supporting a foreign mission. There is no
integrity in a missionary concern that is limited either to foreigners or to fellow citizens. It does not tell the news of
God's act of love for the *whole* world." [16]

The church, then, is always unfinished, and yet it is to be
realized. True loyalty to the gospel always means to let
the Spirit do his creative work. Faithfulness to the word
is not loyalty to a rigid and finished institution, but participation in a creative mission wherein God is at work.

It is one thing to guard the truth that has been entrusted
to us by the Holy Spirit who dwells within us. It is quite
another to let the Spirit enlighten us by imparting wisdom
and making it possible for us to ". . . prove what is the
will of God, what is good and acceptable and perfect." [17]
It is evidence of the Spirit working through the word when
the church constantly attacks new difficulties arising in its
development and when Christians carefully consider with
each other matters that call for discussion in an attitude of
constant prayer and ceaseless listening to the word.

To profess belief in the church is to pledge one's life to Christ in discipleship. Granted that faith must be personal, it is also true that God's redeeming grace through Jesus Christ comes uniquely to men and women when they share in the faith and fellowship. That, in essence, is what the church means.

The Bible as history provides the examples. The Acts of the Apostles and the letters of the apostles represent their ceaseless wrestling with new questions. Unforeseen problems crowded in on every side. Questions were asked, and the answer put in these words, ". . . it has seemed good to the Holy Spirit and to us." [18] The decisions of the apostles were followed by action, not resolutions.

Furthermore, to profess belief in the one, holy, catholic, and apostolic church is not to say that any of the existing churches is in itself the true church of Christ. It is simply to pledge faith and loyalty. We believe in our own churches and traditions insofar as they serve the one true church.

But to claim to belong to the true church is to vow to work and to pray for its fulfillment. It involves the tolerance of a truly catholic spirit, not the sectarian complacency with which the word "tolerance" is too frequently identified. Evangelism and missionary mindedness are among the obvious tests of catholicity. Those who believe in the church should surely be those who desire most eagerly the in-gathering of all mankind into the faith and fellowship.

However, we must never allow ourselves to forget that no mere extension of membership is an adequate aim for believers in the church. The church is not out to get customers or to build up a clientele. The church must penetrate and not merely increase.

Our Lord was relentless about people who covered sea and land to make proselytes for the sake of a self-contained institution. The less the church thinks about itself and the greater its concern for the world that God has redeemed, the more it will be true to its vocation. It will study not only to make more Christians, but so to christen them day by day that in their secular association—whether social, political, or economic—men may recognize Christ as the center of their fellowships.

When we think of the church, our eyes turn at once to Christ, for it is he who is the essence of the church; it is only in him that the church is the church; only in him and through him does it have its function and mission in the gospel. Where Christ is, there is the church. And conversely, where Christ is not, there the church is not. The Church is Christ's Body.

LET THE CHURCH BE ITSELF

Theodore O. Wedel affirms in *The Pulpit Rediscovers Theology:*

The climax of the Gospel is that He [Christ] *does* meet us in personal encounter in the fellowship of the Holy Spirit. He meets us in the Church. His own prophecies are there fulfilled. "Where two or three are gathered in my name, there am I in the midst of them" (Matthew 18:20, RSV). "It is to your advantage that I go away, for if I do not go away, the Comforter will not come unto you." "He shall take of mine, and shall declare it unto you." "I will not leave you desolate; I will come to you." (John 16:7, RSV; 16:14; 14:18).

Here at last, in the life of the fellowship of the Holy Spirit, the paradox of faith and *the* faith, as also the paradox of past and present, and that of the Person of Christ and His work, finds joyous solution. "I believe in the Holy Ghost: the Holy Catholic Church"—this final confession of the historic creeds binds together all that precedes in a living contemporary relationship.[19]

The church witnesses to the unchanging verities—to eternity in the midst of time, to redemption in the midst of sin and corruption, to the love of God triumphant over evil and death itself. The church is the living vehicle of the living Lord, who is very much alive *now*, and rules the world from his position on the right hand of God. It is only as he lives *now* in the church through word and sacrament that the church is the Lord's.

The church is in the world but not of the world. The temptation for the church is either so to separate itself from the world (society) that it has little actual communication with it, or so to identify itself with its present culture that it is no longer able to challenge it. On the one hand, the church, being in the world as Christ's vehicle of redemption, has no choice but to enter into relations with society. In so doing, both the church and society are affected. On the other hand, if the church identifies itself too closely with political, social, or economic systems, it runs the risk of perishing when the systems have run their course.

The church dares never make the truth of the gospel dependent on systems, regimes, or persons. Governments, politics, and culture come and go, but Christ and his church endure forever.

> O where are kings and empires now
> Of old that went and came?

But, Lord, Thy Church is praying yet,
A thousand years the same.

We are in history and we are the makers of history, not spectators. We are on the stage. God will hold us, who are on the world's stage today, accountable for our given part in the unfolding drama. The church must remember that its task is not only to bear witness but also to be the instrument in God's hands in the nation where it has been placed and to the culture to which it both belongs and does not belong.

God will do his work through us if we are open on the Godward side. We sow and water, as St. Paul reminds us, but God alone gives the increase. "My Father is working still, and I am working." [20] We are told of a theological professor in a seminary in Tokyo, Japan, who always addresses two questions to his new students. His first question is, "Do you believe in God?" The answer is invariably a spontaneous "Yes." Then follows the second question, "Do you believe God does anything?" This puzzles them. That God does anything has never occurred to them. The fact that our Lord is at work and that his work includes all men and all the world is a truth that we too frequently forget. Can it be that we become so engrossed and involved in our church plans and activities that we go forth on our own? Our Lord tells us to tarry—to come apart with him—and we rush to our work ill-prepared. He tells us to go forth and witness to him, and we linger and are ineffective. We fail the second because we are not obedient to the first. The church cannot possibly be the church unless the word of Christ dwells in it richly, and unless the church goes forth on its mission under the commitment of that word.

When the church is so committed, it can assess the spiritual and moral aspects of the changes that are taking place. Are they constructive or destructive? Do they confuse means and ends? Do they deny or affirm the worth of the individual soul?

A properly oriented church can say, "Thus saith the Lord." It will declare that man is not made for machines; the machines are made for man—for every man. Man is not made for the industrial order; the industrial order is made for man—for every man. Man is not made for the political order; the political order is made for man—for every man. The church itself must be so sure of eternal values that it can put the right price tags on the commodities and orders of life.

The world, impermanent as it is, is God's world. Here we must ". . . work the works of him who sent us" while it is day; "night comes, when no one can work." [21] We need not lose heart or panic because of the threatening clouds, because we look ". . . forward to the city which has foundations." [22]

On the other hand, as long as we have life all the aspects of this world's life become an opportunity for making known the will of him who is Lord of both heaven and earth. The other-worldly dimensions of our faith do not relax our stewardship for this impermanent earth; it is rather intensified. The Christian hope does not free us from responsibilities to the earth; it only adds worth and meaning to all the tasks of earth. Elevated to the high station of citizenship in the eternal kingdom, we turn earthward under daily compulsion into all of life. Only by having our destiny lifted above the ever-changing eddies of this world's transient successes and failures can we begin to live fruitfully and without fear.

"On Holy Errand"

The church is on a continuing holy *errand*. So is the congregation—the Body of Christ in your community—where you are a member. And so are you!

It is on *holy* errand, for the Lord of the Church is holy! To His Church and members He gives holy orders about the errand. It is one holy errand "until He comes."

Wherever a Christian is, he is on "the holy errand." In whatever neighborhood a congregation is it has an "holy errand." In every community that is unchurched or underchurched a church must be planted—to be on holy errand! [23]

3:

WE WHO ARE
THE UNITED STATES

Whatever our racial or national origin, we share a common humanity. We must eat and work and sleep. We marry and have children. We vote and pay taxes. If we live long enough, we grow old. Sooner or later, death comes to us all. We bring nothing with us into the world and we take nothing out. Regardless of origin we share such common occupations as farming, selling, science, law, the ministry, and carpentry. We depend on one another both to produce and to maintain.

WHO ARE WE?

When we talk about Americans, about whom are we talking? We are all kinds of people. We come from all the continents and nations of the earth, as well as from all the islands of the seas. We are white and black and brown and yellow and red, and all the shades in between. The United States has been called the land of many faces. Our country is overwhelmingly rich in the variety of people within her borders.

Some 160 million Americans are white. But white people represent a wide variety. They are of Swiss, Dutch, German,

English, Irish, Swedish, Polish, Spanish, Italian, Greek, Hungarian, and all other Caucasian origins. Their cultures, mores, and customs have been woven into the woof and fabric of our American life. Within the respective nationalities there are marked differences—people who have been Americans for many generations and recent arrivals rich and poor, skilled and unskilled, good and bad.

The 17 million Negro Americans have cultural and national backgrounds that differ as much as those of white people. Millions of them have their roots deep in American life and history. They, too, have lived, fought, and died for the country we all love. In music, art, literature, education, sports, and science they have made contributions quite beyond their opportunities. They, too, have been and are the makers of America.

There are the million or more Chinese and Japanese people who share common citizenship as Americans. Among them, too, there are varied cultural patterns and customs. There are wide differences, for instance, in the languages and habits of Mandarin speaking Chinese and the Cantonese. People from the Orient have contributed an added dimension to American life.

More than 40 per cent of the 12 million Jewish people of the world live in the United States, and some 40 per cent of these make their home in New York City. These Americans have rich traditions, close family ties, and they are people with a sense of destiny.

There are the first Americans—the Indians. This country has always been their homeland, and here they have chosen to remain. They, too, represent a mixture of cultures. They are of many tribes, all with their distinctive customs. Once they were called the vanishing Americans, and their number reached a low of 250,000. Today they number approximately six hundred thousand. Once they lived almost entirely on reservations. Today they are in all parts of the country. E. Russell Carter has graphically portrayed the Indian American's contribution in *The Gift is Rich*.[1]

When Alaska gained statehood—officially proclaimed on January 3, 1959—191,000 people were added to the population of the United States. Seventeen thousand are Eskimos, 16,000 are Indians, and 5,000 are Aleuts who live in the extreme west of Alaska and on the Aleutian Islands.

The last territory to achieve statehood was Hawaii. Who are these Hawaiian Americans? One estimate is that 34 per cent are Japanese in origin, 35 per cent Hawaiian and part Hawaiian, 12 per cent Filipino, 6 per cent Puerto Rican, one per cent Korean. It is reported that one out of three marriages in Hawaii is between members of different ethnic groups.

"It appears that in Hawaii the problem of race has been solved in a more satisfactory manner than anywhere in the world," is the opinion of Bishop W. Vernon Middleton in *Methodism in Alaska and Hawaii*. "While it cannot be maintained," he continues, "that race prejudice has been abolished, it is certainly at a minimum. . . . You may visit the offices of any public utility and find there employees of all races working beside each other and being paid the same amount for the same job. . . . It is not an uncommon thing to have two Orientals and two Caucasians as vice-presidents of the same bank. There is no single racial group which is numerically strong enough to dominate the others." [2]

Between 1945 and the end of 1959, some 666,000 Puerto

Ricans exercised their privilege of establishing residence in the states. The major cities, particularly in the East, have claimed most of these people. Many of them are among the most industrious of our citizens, but they and the children who have been born to them on the mainland are finding adjustment to our way of living difficult.

And there are the recent immigrants. They include the DP's, the refugees, and all who have come in under the Immigration Act. Between 1950 and 1959 their number totaled 2,499,268. They have come from Europe, Asia, South America, Africa, Central America, Canada, Mexico—from all continents and climes. They have brought with them their skills, their gift of language and culture and experience that contribute to the rich mosaic of our country. America is complex and confusing to these immigrants—particularly the American city where most of them settle. Common to all immigrants, in all countries, is the difficulty experienced with new ways of life, with new language for most of them, and often with racial and national prejudice.

How peculiar we are! We like to travel to other cities and states—to foreign lands, if we can—to see how people live. We delight to talk about strange customs we come across. We enjoy movies and TV shows that introduce us to people whose ways are different from ours. We are happy to welcome "foreigners" as speakers at our PTA and parish meetings. Yet we tend to close our eyes to the exciting possibilities all around us for the enrichment of our lives and churches. What are these exciting possibilities? People, of course! People of a nationality different from ours, a color lighter or darker, a homeland origin as dear to them as ours is to us, a heritage of customs, holidays, menus—at first strange, then fascinating. On your street, across town, or down your road there's someone worth knowing—not because you have so much in common, but because there's something uncommon about a lot of folks. He is one of us —a fellow American.

WHERE DO WE LIVE?

It is hard to say where we live. We are here today and gone tomorrow. We have become a nation of nomads. Mobility continues at the rate of 30 million people a year. Twenty per cent of city people move annually, 17 per cent of the people in rural areas, and 22 per cent of those in exurbia.

It was Hermann Morse, the home mission statesman of the United Presbyterian Church, U.S.A., who said there is nothing new about the high rate of mobility in American history. The population movement westward, southward, northward —the geographical frontier movement—was one of the forces that made possible the evangelization of America.

Nevertheless the present population mobility is vastly different. It whirls people together by the sheer agitation of economic necessity and opportunity. It shuffles and reshuffles people of varied races and cultures. It concentrates people in urban regions. The uprooting of people, the influx of people of different cultural and racial heritages, the fear of new neighbors, the very conflict of cultures cause anxiety and tension all over the country. Those who move feel a sense of lostness and those who stay experience lostness because the community "just isn't the same any more."

The white people are moving in all directions, with the general trend toward the west, the south, and the southwest.

The Negro population is moving northward, almost exclusively into the cities. In 1940 the Negro population in Washington, D.C., was 28.5 per cent of the total and today it is 54 per cent (in the capital city of our country the whites are the minority); in Gary, Ind., it was 18.3 per cent in 1940, and today is 37 per cent; in Newark, N.J., 10.8 per cent in 1940, and today 36 per cent; in Chicago, Ill., 8.3 per cent in 1940, and today 24 per cent; in Los Angeles, Calif., 6 per cent in 1940, and today 12 per cent. New York City officials have forecast that by 1970 Negroes and Puerto Ricans will constitute 45 per cent of the population of Manhattan and nearly one third of the entire city. An increasing number of white people are also moving from southern rural communities, particularly from the southern Appalachian states, to northern cities. The vast majority of these Negroes and whites are Protestants. As Protestants we can no longer point to the inner city as being primarily the responsibility of the Roman Catholics—if ever we could!

We are all on the move. From rural areas to the city, from inner city to the suburb and back again, from north to south, south to north, east to west, and west to east, Puerto Rico to New York, from reservations to cities and small towns.

As the population of the United States continues to gravitate in ever increasing numbers to the larger metropolitan areas, tremendous changes are inevitable—changes that exert forceful impact on the people and institutions within these communities. While the expansion of the cities outward continues unabated, there has grown a new frontier that moves not outward but inward into existing communities. These two related movements are what Hermann N. Morse calls the "centralizing and decentralizing trend."

Most of us live in the 168 areas that the United States census recognizes as metropolitan. We live downtown, in the inner city, in the "gray zone," on the gold coast, in the residental neighborhood, in the suburb, or in scattered non-farm communities beyond the suburbs. We live in hotels, in rooming houses, in luxury apartments, and in other multiple dwelling places of assorted types, above stores, in basements, in mansions, in ranch houses, in bungalows, in trailers.

The emergence of the gigantic super-cities, crazy-quilt mixtures of city and suburb, of slum and factory, of ranch house and skyscraper, of shopping center and expressway, poses many problems. Three problems are dominant—immigration, housing, and planning.

Increased production increases the demand for labor. In days past immigrants from Europe supplied the demand. That day is largely gone. Industry today has turned to four sources of cheap labor—the Negroes, the Mexicans, the Puerto Ricans, and the "southern whites." These new recruits face two problems that former immigrants faced. They come principally from rural communities and are unprepared for the complex urban culture, and because of their manners and mores they are held in contempt by the larger community. In addition they must settle in inner city neighborhoods that are already run down and in dwellings that are disreputable. Add to this the fact that the Negroes, Puerto Ricans, and Mexicans are the object of racial discrimination.

It is obvious that the housing problem is closely related to the immigration problem. Writing some months ago in *The New York Times Magazine*, Edward J. Logue suggested that some real concerns would develop if people would visit slums to face at first hand the filth and misery in which many people must exist.

A representative of The American Council to Improve Our Neighborhood comments:

Even if there were no humanitarian, religious, or ethical motives for removing these eyesores from our communities, there would still be compelling economic reasons. America cannot afford slums. *You* cannot afford slums. Your money is at stake. Your money, your health, your well-being. Disease breeds there. Crime festers there. Delinquency stems from there. And disease, and crime, and delinquency, and vice stretch their grimy tentacles far out from the slums. Every homeowner, renter, and landlord has a personal stake in his own city's slums. So does everyone else—every taxpayer, businessman, industrialist, builder, city planner, and public official.

Social scientists tell us that people are influenced in the formation of their opinions and habits from 60 per cent to 90 per cent by their environment. The sick sections of the cities—large and small—are growing. The church cannot hope to bring the whole gospel to the whole man unless it is actually involved in helping to change the environment. Directly and indirectly many voices are pleading for the churches to assume the role they have always claimed—that of being moral and spiritual centers of communities that, without such leadership, are confused, disorganized, drifting, and lost.

Suburbs and communities beyond the suburbs are the new urban frontiers. The trend to the suburbs has been, and continues to be, phenomenal. As New Yorkers have been pushing up into Westchester County, out to Long Island, across into New Jersey, so outlying cities such as Boston,

Philadelphia, Washington, Detroit, Chicago, Dallas, Houston, Tucson, Miami, Minneapolis, Kansas City, Denver, San Francisco, Los Angeles, and Seattle have experienced phenomenal growth. Land that once was used for farming is now covered by acres of homes. Little villages on the fringes of our cities have been transformed into large, bustling communities. Old established suburbs have doubled, tripled or quadrupled in population. Some have become satellite cities of 25,000, 50,000, and even 100,000 population.

There is a tendency to throw all suburbs into one hopper. We know, of course, there are different kinds of suburbs— a kind of segregation by status. There are rich suburbs and poor suburbs. There are suburbs made up largely of the foreign born and those that have sizable Negro populations. There are suburbs for the workers as well as suburbs for top organization men. There are Cadillac suburbs and suburbs where the Chevrolet or Ford is predominant. There are suburbs with growing areas of slums and others that are "spanking new."

Tunnard and Reed point out:

Too often we forget that the suburb has been built at a terrifying cost. This lies not primarily in the *loss of the countryside* before the lengthening superhighway and spreading development; that is perhaps inevitable in the face of a growing population and the very natural desire of the American to own his own home. Rather it lies in *the abandonment of the city*, the center of our civilization. Like the Mad Hatter at the tea party, who moved around the table using only the clean teacups and leaving the dirty ones behind him, we Americans move on to new land once we have exploited the old. The central city has seemingly been worked for all that it is worth and then aban-

doned for the suburban fringe. What is perhaps more frighten-
ing is that the suburban fringe of twenty-five or fifteen years
ago is, in its turn, being worn out.[3]

Some harmony must come out of the gigantic industrial
and economic forces at work within and around the urban
centers. Furthermore, the flight from industrialization has
proved to be an impossible cause. What was yesterday's
dream house or apartment becomes a building in today's
rehabilitated neighborhood and tomorrow's slums. We know
by now, or ought to know, that the division between city
and suburb is largely a myth. Is not the suburb just in a
different part of the city?

The question to be resolved is how to achieve balance
between redevelopment, conservation, and new development. This means planning. The problems connected with
metropolitan planning are certainly as much, if not more, the
problems and concerns of the church as they are of any
other institution, private or public. The problems of the city
are the problems of the people. What we need is a penetrating understanding of the total city and the courage to face
people rather than faceless issues.

In addition, there are the wheeled suburbs. More than
three million Americans—two thirds of them skilled workers, professionals, and retired people—now live in the more
than thirteen thousand trailer courts. The wheeled boxes
they call home are more house than van: all have a living
room, one or two bedrooms, a kitchen, and a bath; many
have such embellishments as fireplaces and picture windows.
The bulk of the people who live in them stay more put than
they do in many apartment areas. The average mobile home
owner now remains rooted to one park for at least two

years. The 1950 shipments of trailers from over two hundred manufacturers came close to being 10 per cent of all the private homes started in the United States that year. Since 1950, the number of trailers in use as housing has climbed steadily from an estimated 500,000 to about 1,400,000. Within the trailer industry there is serious concern today about the woeful state of parks and the problem of getting better ones constructed. Most communities are laggard in evolving a rational, democratic policy for dealing with trailer parks. What communities are probably going to have to do, soon, is tackle realistically the problem of parks by requiring them to conform to some meaningful standards, for trailer dwelling can be expected to persist, and its problems must be met by planners and architects and churches.

Rural America is in an extraordinary flux. A new rural society is emerging. On the one hand there are the rural communities that are oriented toward the cities and are actually within the orbit of the cities. On the other hand there are the thousands of rural communities, geographically removed from the cities, that are experiencing social upheaval. More and more the people of these communities are engaged in non-farm or part-time non-farm employment. If the new "hybrid" society is to be productive of good it needs the co-operative work and concern of churchmen, economists, and sociologists. The faithfulness of the church in this area, as has been suggested by E. W. Mueller, director of town and country work for the National Lutheran Council, is a part of its stewardship of the gospel.

Many town and country communities are discouraged because of population losses caused by mechanized farming. Dr. Otto G. Hoiberg of the University of Nebraska insists that the population loss does not necessarily mean that a community is waning.[4] Fortunately there is no inherent relation, he states, between the quality of community living and the size of population. During the nineteenth century when the little country of Denmark was passing through a most difficult period of her history, a slogan was born that urged the Danes to convert outward loss to inner gain. In our church life, too, we need to realize that not more congregations, but more effective congregations are needed.

William H. Lazareth rightly says:

City planning, urban renewal, housing developments, industrial expansion, commercialization of agriculture, convergence of rural and urban areas, and the social disintegration of family and home life—these are all part of the actual 'flesh' in which the living Word must become incarnate. Public officials are rightly impatient with impractical, starry-eyed Utopians who know nothing of the political facts of life. But they do understand the language of gadgets, tenements, slums, crime, delinquency, highways, saloons, race riots, and populations trends.[5]

GOD'S PLAN FOR AMERICA

In the face of population explosion, shuffling and reshuffling of people, broken relationships, race and class prejudice, is the church committed to being the church, or is it resigned to being simply another social institution? Are people—all people—the church's passion, as people were and are the passion of the church's Lord? Does evangelism set our feet and money into the inner cities, into the crowded apartment areas, out to the lonely outposts, into haunts of wretchedness and misery, into the industrial communities, as well as into the suburbs? Is the task of evangelism one of reconciliation? Are walls broken down and enmities healed? What costly steps are the churches taking to heal the deep hurts of bigotry, hate, loneliness, lostness? Can it be that the church contributes, time and again, to the hurts of people as well as to the fragmentation of community?

We are apt to think that the early church was made up of a small band of people with very much the same experiences and culture. However, if we reread the book of Acts we will quickly discover that a glorious mix-up resulted from the outpouring of the Holy Spirit on the day of Pentecost.

When the Spirit of God moved the hearts of the listeners as well as those of the apostles, people of sixteen nationalities and three continents were baptized into the Christian church and made members of the fellowship of the Holy Spirit. Across the diversity of language, color, custom, and culture the will of God cut sharply, and three thousand new members of the church rejoiced in their experience of real unity.

It was no accident that God chose such a motely crowd on which to bestow his gifts of faith, cleansing, and brotherly love. Pentecost was a mighty demonstration of his purpose ". . . that they may all be one." It was the undoing of Babel which had sent the tribes of men stumbling along their separate and quarrelsome ways.[6]

St. Luke describes the mixed collection with the telling sentence, "Now the company of those who believed were of one heart and soul." [7]

May it not be in God's plan for the nations that America is intended to be a demonstration to our troubled and fragmented world that men of every kind can live together creatively and hopefully and equably? That demonstration

God looks for in his Church, which is the Body of Christ. This demonstration will not be given unless the local congregation, as well as the Church Universal, is the fellowship of the Holy Spirit—a fellowship that knows nothing about the limitations of nationality, race, color, class, education, social status, or economic circumstance.

We may adore God for his love and thank him for the grace of the Lord Jesus Christ, but we seem to have trouble with the fellowship of the Holy Spirit. We like to keep our religion as a purely personal affair. But we cannot be true to the Christian gospel and escape its horizontal applications. We have to take the word "fellowship" seriously. We must accept the idea that this word expresses the serious will of the heart of God, whose constant intention it is to join together what the devil has put asunder.

We are told that when Goya, the artist, was aged and in exile in Bordeaux, he would ask people in the cafes to drop three crumbs at random on a piece of paper and then, however remote or awkwardly separated these might be, he never failed to draw a figure with its head and hands where the crumbs had been. This is something like what the Spirit of God is trying to do on the canvas of the world and on the canvas of the community. He's endeavoring to establish a connection among the isolated crumbs of humanity, and at the same time to draw a picture that turns out to be the Body of Christ.

We recognize and practice, as it were, the fellowship on the world-wide level. Missionaries are sent to all parts of the earth. The sticky application, however, is on the local level—the congregation. There we often tend to draw the line. And yet, only there is its integrity validated. To be united with others in the fellowship of the church is not only to be knit together with fellow Christians in Africa, China, India, South America, and other lands, but to be joined as well with men of different color and social status in our own country and in our immedtate community who also acknowledge Christ as Lord and Savior.

God's love is not conditioned on any social, cultural, or racial pattern. Careful pickings and choosings, likes and dislikes, race prejudice, class prejudice, and all the rest must certainly look silly in the glow of the one God and Father of us all, in whom we live and move and have our being. The Christian faith recognizes no special right, privilege, duty, immunity, or limitation based upon race or nationality. The Scriptures do not even take cognizance of race as such. They do, however, clearly teach the unity of the whole human family. Men are not to be accepted because they fit some arbitrary norm or can be placed readily in the compartments of existing church strategy. They are to be taken and loved and witnessed to as they are.

Our purpose is not, therefore, that other people join us in our churches. It is rather that we and they so respond to God's self-giving love in Jesus Christ that we are together the people of God— "And this is not your own doing, it is the gift of God, not because of works, lest any man should boast." [8] In this way, and in this way alone, all people become one people.

4:

CANADA COMES
INTO ITS OWN

*T*he twentieth century is Canada's." With this crisp sentence Russell Hurst began a feature article in *The Minneapolis Tribune*, June 13, 1955.

Consider the facts:

Among the world's largest countries, Canada is second only to Russia. Its area is about 3,800,000 square miles compared to 3,600,000 roughly for the United States including Alaska and Hawaii.

Relatively speaking, Canada is sparsely populated, with less than five people per square mile, compared to about fifty per square mile for the United States.

Canada leads the world in fresh-water area, vital to transportation and power generation. The St. Lawrence Seaway system is navigable for more than 2,000 miles. Even longer is the Mackenzie River system, navigable for more than 2,600 miles through the Northwest Territories to the Arctic Ocean.

Only a third of Canada's total area has been brought under development to date. Less than 8 per cent of the country is classed as occupied farmland; an equal area, at present unoccupied, is considered suitable for agriculture. About 24 per cent of the total area is regarded as productive timber-land, and about two thirds of this is accessible presently.

There are vast resources in the Northwest Territories and the roads-to-resources program has gotten under way. All told, government and private spending in the northern "wilds" is expected to approach one billion dollars in the next ten years.

Bruce Hutchison, one of Canada's native sons and a pro-lific writer, has referred to his land as the unknown country. It is an apt designation. Who knows this country's potential in terms of natural wealth? How soon will there be a minor population explosion in the presently remote northern out-posts? Who knows but that this country may be the Canaan for millions of dispossessed people? Canada is a vast ware-house of untouched wealth, still in the era of pioneer strength. The friendly doors of this great land are open to the enterprising hopeless of the world.

Until after World War II the vast territories to the north were thought to be nothing more than a land of bush and tundra and rock and snow—a wasteland that could support only a few hardy folk and that had little or nothing to offer the Canadian economy.

What amazing changes have taken place in recent years! Wasteland is being converted into wealth—oil, nickel, iron ore, uranium, and gold are available in prodigious quantities, Kitimat, Sept Iles, Arvida, Moak Lake, and Uranium City pinpoint some of the areas of development and indicate the northern thrust of Canada's people in recent years.

The "Publisher's Letter" in *Time*, September 24, 1956, quotes Canada desk man Art White, as follows: "It is not enough to have correspondents in the centers of population (in Canada); more and more significant news is being made out in the bush, in mining towns in tough, hard-to-reach areas where men are digging, farming, lumbering. . . ."

There is adventure ahead for Canadians and Canadians-to-be in helping to lay the groundwork for towns and cities of tomorrow. Concerning the future of the Northwest Territories, R. G. Robertson, commissioner of these territories, predicts that there will not be large cities like those of the south. He feels that there will probably be only a few centers of 50,000 or so in the Yukon and the Mackenzie Valley, the focal points of road and rail facilities. But over most of the north there will be scattered communities of a thousand to 15,000 population that have grown up around mines.

As has been indicated, areas that were backward a decade ago now contain thriving mineral towns, shipping points, exploration centers. Such major cities as Ottawa, Montreal, Toronto, Winnipeg, Regina, Edmonton, Saskatoon, Calgary, and Vancouver are bursting at the seams with growing population. Not only are there thriving, bustling new communities and bulging, booming cities, but even the oldest parts of Canada are experiencing face lifting—urban renewal. An excellent example of urban renewal is the Regent Park Housing Project in Toronto. From Montreal to Windsor—the St. Lawrence Seaway band—"strip cities" are beginning to connect one major city with the other.

FASCINATING STOPPING OFF PLACES

Here are some fascinating stopping off places for those who are contemplating an east-west trip through Canada; Corner Brook, the paper and pulp city of Newfoundland;

the shipping outlet harbor town of Sept Iles in Quebec with its automatic docks; Schefferville mining center, rising in the wilderness to tap vast Quebec-Labrador ore reserves; Arvida, Quebec, the world's largest aluminum producing center; Uranium City, the new outpost of the atomic age; Yellow Knife, of the Northwest Territories, jumping off place for mining development, near huge deposits of gold, silver, copper, and lead; White Horse, the doorway to the Yukon, expected to become the center for economic empire based on mining, power, and timber; and Kitimat, British Columbia, site of one of the world's largest, most modern aluminum plants.

More than seven million people from the United States spend all or part of their vacations in Canada each year, according to the Canadian Government Travel Bureau. It is estimated that three fourths of them have been there before. They pour over the border, mostly by car, to fish, hunt, and ski; to relax at lake or seaside resorts; to visit relatives and friends. No doubt many of them simply want to drive around and have a look at the country.

THE PEOPLE OF CANADA

From the beginning Canada was a mixture of peoples—Indian and Eskimo. The first immigrants to arrive were the early traders, chiefly English and French—still today the two basic national stocks. Some forty thousand Empire Loyalists came from the American colonies while those colonies were gaining their independence from Britain. The great immigration waves have taken place just prior to World War I and since World War II. Of the approximately 18 million people about 39 per cent are of British

origin and 25 per cent of French stock, forming two subor-
dinate nationalisms within a super-nationalism. There are
155,000 Indians and 11,000 Eskimos. The remainder of the
population have their origins in all nations and races; pre-
dominating and in their order are German, Ukrainian, Scandinavian, Dutch, Polish, Jewish, Italian, Russian. Of the total
number of immigrants in 1958—124,851 in all—26,622 came
from the United Kingdom, 28,564 from Italy, 14,449 from
Germany, 10,846 from the United States, 7,595 from the
Netherlands, and 5,418 from Greece. The remainder came
from some forty other countries. The youthful character of
the immigrants is demonstrated by the fact that almost half
of them were from twenty to thirty-four years of age. The
majority of immigrants today head for the industrialized
areas. In 1956, of the 165,000 emigrating to Canada, over
90,000 settled in Ontario, most of them in and around Toronto.

THE MOOD OF CANADA

Along the almost four thousand mile Canadian-U.S.A.
border there is no fort nor cannon, no secret police. There
are rivalries to be sure, commercial and cultural, but in all
the annals of history there has never before been such a symbol of good will and trust between nations as this border.

Bruce Hutchison has called Canada one of the most complex, brittle, and confusing nations in the world—its people
proud, sensitive, and easily offended.

As I visit Canada—two or three times each year—I get
the impression that Canada is neither pro U.S.A. nor pro
British; rather it is pro Canada. This is something that people
of the United States should both learn and appreciate.

Writes Joseph Barber in *Good Fences Make Good Neighbors*, "If it is possible to generalize about attitudes perhaps one may say that, while Canadians have reservations about individual Britishers, they ardently support British institutions and British concepts of justice. On the other hand, Canadians feel at home with individual Americans and understand and like them, but are wary of what they conceive to be American 'values,' and the 'American way of life'." [1]

Canada is experiencing the growing pains of a small—in population, though not in geography—nation gradually gaining status among the nations of the world. There is emerging a national consciousness, coupled with a natural self-consciousness. Eager to be itself, the country is little by little developing a Canadian style of life. Canadian political and economic leaders are disturbed by the hold that American culture has on their society, and that too is understandable, since there cannot be a Canadian style of life without a Canadian point of view. The editor of *MacLean's Magazine* gave expression to this in an editorial about ten years ago:

> For more than a hundred years this country struggled, for the most part bloodlessly, to cease being a British colony. Now many of its inhabitants are afraid that their country will spend the next hundred years struggling, also bloodlessly, to avoid becoming a colony of the United States. We do not fear a physical conquest. We do not fear forcible absorption. But we know the conquest is already half achieved, the absorption well begun. [2]

It is certainly not clear what national image the people of Canada are trying to bring into focus. At the moment, as has been stated, they are experiencing growing pains.

It is perilous to indicate trends even in one's own country, let alone the trends of another country. Risky as it is, an interpretation of Canada must be attempted if we are to understand the country and our Canadian friends.

Political Trends

There is no doubt that there is a growing sense of nationalism that distinguishes sharply between Canadianism and Americanism. The border is like a hedge between neighboring yards—not unfriendly, but a real dividing line.

Canada is increasing in prominence and influence among the nations of the world, as seen in its relation to the United Nations and the role it plays as a member nation. It is interesting to note also that in 1935 Canada was represented abroad only in the United Kingdom, the United States, France, and Japan; but by 1955 it had diplomatic representation in forty-seven different countries, nearly all the major lands of the world.

Sociological Trends

There is a positive devotion to dualism as a way of life in Canada. Both French and English are official languages. Railroads are under public as well as private ownership. So are airlines. Crown corporations carry on flourishing business alongside private companies. Of the fifty television stations, eight are owned and operated by the Canadian Broadcasting Company, an agency of the Canadian Government. Radio stations are also both publicly and privately owned. In the Province of Quebec there is a dual system of public education under the support and direction of the state. The Roman Catholic system is almost entirely French. The Protestant system is almost entirely English.[3]

There has been and continues to be a substantial annual growth in population: from 14 to about 18 million since 1951; (approximately 3 per cent annually) with an anticipated 22½ million by 1970. Urban centers have shown a phenomenal growth, with dense population concentrated in an otherwise sparsely populated land. The urbanward movement is indicated by the fact that the total population increased 14.8 per cent between 1951 and 1956, but the rural population increased only 3.4 per cent. The urban population increased over this period at the rate of 21.5, to reach 10,714,855. In 1956, nearly 6,300,000 persons lived in the fifteen metropolitan areas—more than a third of the total population and close to 60 per cent of the urban population. As for the fifteen metropolitan areas, the increase in the area was 19.3 per cent, in the city proper 9 per cent, and in the suburban area 41.7 per cent. In 1958, 67 per cent of the population was urban; the urban population acceleration will continue. Reports seem to indicate that the mobility of population in Canada approximates that of the United States.

Southern Ontario since the end of World War II has become one of the major industrial areas of the world, and the opening of the St. Lawrence Seaway should bring another tremendous expansion to Canada's industrial center. Despite all attempts by the Canadian Government to direct "New Canadians" into farming, most of them settle in the cities, particularly in the Toronto metropolitan area.

The birth rate in Canada is among the highest in the world —approximately 29 per thousand of population. Life expectancy increased from 61 in 1931 to 70.5 years in 1956. Immigration continues strong. Early immigration was from Germany, the Scandinavian countries, and the British Isles. More recently there has been a substantial increase in the number of immigrants from other countries—from Italy, the Netherlands, and Greece in particular.

A troublesome and costly problem in Canadian cities today is traffic congestion. There are about five million cars, trucks, and buses in the country, half of them traveling twenty billion miles a year on only twenty thousand miles of city streets. It is estimated that by 1980, Canada's urban population will be twenty-one million people and the city streets will bear the weight of fourteen million motorized vehicles.

Economic Trends

Dr. James R. Mutchmor, secretary of the Board of Evangelism and Social Service of the United Church of Canada, observes:

Canada has grown up. Hers is a vigorous and prosperous life, with the gross national product, employment, trade, drinking, gambling, car ownership, building, retail sales, travel and almost every other index of economic and social life at record high levels. Canada has matured rapidly. Her record in the two great wars of this century, her leadership at the United Nations and her sense of strength and destiny have served to give her a new and even strident feeling of mastery and power . . . depressed places are but tiny spots on a heavily prosperous map.

Forest products, a varied lot of valuable commodities led by newsprint, now top Canada's export list. Vast new mineral discoveries have been made in the near and far north. Oil wells multiply in Alberta and British Columbia. Gas flows in national and subsidiary pipelines. Canada's uranium mines are among the world's richest producers of this magic metal. To cap all this, the central industries heartland of the nation is crossed by the newly opened Atlantic Seaway carrying ocean shipping to Port Arthur and Fort William . . . a new political, industrial and social era has begun. . . . The nation is on the move.[4]

Canada is presently the fifth trading nation of the world. In an address on May 19, 1960, Mr. John C. Pallett, parliamentary secretary to the Minister of Trade and Commerce, pointed out that Canadians have created a highly productive nation, although major production is concentrated in about 15 or 20 per cent of the country, and that they must now look to the 80 per cent that stretches to the north, as important today as their West was in 1867.[5]

THE CHURCHES OF CANADA

Sectarianism never reached the same proportions in Canada as in the United States. There are only some thirty separate denominations listed in the Canadian census, whereas over three hundred are listed as active denominations in the *Handbook of Denominations in the United States.*

Forty-three per cent of the people are Roman Catholics, at least nominally. The United Church of Canada has 20 per cent of the population as adherents, and 15 per cent belong to the Anglican Church. Most of the remaining Protestants belong to Presbyterian, Baptist, Lutheran, and Mennonite churches. The churches of Canada, like the churches of the United States, are faced with their country's rapid expansion and growth, mobility and urbanization, as well as waning population in many rural communities. More immigrants, more babies, more new homes, more activity in the Northland mean more churches, and who can estimate the future now that the new seaway is completed? The growing pains of church extension are common—pains that include the skyrocketing cost of sites and expensive first units.

The churches of Canada are well aware that planting missions in the suburbs and the Northland is but one phase— though a most important one—of their total witness. Two million immigrants have come to Canada in the last decade. Reaching out to and integrating these newcomers, who represent 10 per cent of the nation's population, is not easy. There are the downtowns of the cities, the inner city areas, the apartment communities, the sections undergoing renewal or for which renewal is planned. Critical days have come upon many rural communities and therefore upon their churches. The churches are challenged to re-examine their position and strategy.

THE CHURCHES IN CO-OPERATION

There are two national councils of churches—the Canadian Council of Churches and the Canadian Lutheran Council. There is no official relationship between the two, but there are good informal relationships and co-operation. None of the Lutheran bodies are affiliated with the Canadian Council of Churches, but the United Lutheran Church in America is "in friendly association" with it. All the Lutheran bodies are members of the Canadian Lutheran Council except the Lutheran Church Missouri Synod. In the States three Lutheran bodies have membership in the National Council of Churches, and the Lutheran Church Missouri Synod is a member of its Division of Home Missions.

The member churches of the Canadian Council of Churches are the Anglican, United, Presbyterian, Greek Orthodox, Russian Orthodox, Greek Catholic, Churches of Christ (Disciples), Evangelical United Brethren, Reformed Episcopal, Society of Friends, Salvation Army (a denomination in Canada), and the Baptist Federation.[6]

The *Record of Proceedings* of the Canadian Council of Churches, published bi-annually, has no reports on home missions. One of the anomalous aspects of the council is that it has departments of ecumenical affairs, evangelism, Christian education, overseas missions, and social relations—but no department of home missions. Occasionally conferences are called to discuss specific home mission concerns, but there is no co-operative research, no co-operative planning.

In reply to some inquiries concerning the work of the Canadian Council of Churches, Dr. W. J. Gallagher, general secretary, stated:

We have no department of home missions because the home mission boards of the churches, at a conference we had with them some time ago, decided that they do not need or do not want such a co-operative organization at present. They asked us instead to arrange for conferences on home mission problems from time to time, and this we do. Such a conference is now planned for this November. We have a Committee on Church Extension, but it has accomplished little to date beyond two very useful conferences on this matter. We have a Committee on Christian Stewardship, which has been very effective in promoting "sector" campaigns, but has not given special attention to rural problems.

To keep the record straight, it must be pointed out that the Canadian Council of Churches came into being because it was felt that the churches ". . . should have something to say on the direction and goals of a continuing industrial revolution, so much more dangerous for the human race in view of the latest scientific discoveries." [7] However, unless the member bodies are willing to work out a co-ordinated program of mission to Canada it is doubtful that the council will make a significant impact on Canadian national life. It would appear that the Preamble to the Constitution of the council should make this desirable: "Believing that we are one in faith in our Lord Jesus Christ, the incarnate Word of God, and in allegiance to Him as Head of the Church. . . ."

The Canadian Lutheran Council has a division of Canadian missions, and its five Regional Home Mission Committees meet at least semi-annually to allocate fields for new missions.[8] Concern for a united witness was expressed by the Augustana Lutheran Church at its convention in 1960 when it adopted the following resolution: "The Church memorializes the Canadian Lutheran Council to consider the possibility of devising a structure for co-operative planning on the part of all evangelical Protestants."

There are gigantic challenges that face the Protestant churches of Canada. Co-operatively they need to pool their research resources and pool their programs in order that they may present a united witness. Canada is on the march and the churches must learn to march together. This cannot happen if denominations insist on pursuing their own way. The sickness of the inner cities, duplicating ministries in waning rural communities, the push to the North, suburban expansion, the witness to the immigrant population, the promise of Canada's future, and the limited resources of men and funds make co-operative planning a must.

5:

CHURCHES FOR
TODAY'S FRONTIERS

Granted that thousands of churches must be planted in this decade, will they be "new" churches dedicated to the extension of the kingdom of God, or will they be cut from the patterns of yesterday's churches? Will they take communities in stride in their witness and service? Will they be cells of the Body of Christ? Will they be competitive or will they present a united witness? Will they be established where they are needed, or will opportunism determine church extension strategy? Will the Protestant denominations expand in terms of new outposts or will they succeed for the most part only in moving the church from one place to another? Will they be committed to witnessing both on a broad front and in depth?

These are not rhetorical questions!

Many suburban communities are already overchurched. For instance, one such community, with a population of one thousand, has six Protestant churches and a Roman Catholic Church.

A seven-year-old suburban church is in process of relocation because people of a different race are moving in. A so-called new mission recently relocated, leaving in its wake a spiritual vacuum. An editorial in a daily newspaper rebuked a congregation less than ten years old for abandoning a community desperately in need of the church. A church built at a cost of $110,000 eleven years ago is for sale—Puerto Ricans have moved into the community.

A jurisdictional administrator reported that while seventy-six congregations were established in his area during the last decade, the net increase of congregations was only eleven. Five congregations were involved in mergers, twenty relocated, and forty were dissolved.

Some months ago I talked to the manager of a large housing project, financed by one of the old line insurance companies. I asked, "How did this company dare to risk such a large investment in this area?" His reply was, "No thanks are due the churches. When the community experienced change they fled like scared rabbits. Had it not been for a Jewish hospital and a technical college that decided not only to stay but to expand their facilities, this company would never have made the investment. After all, they must protect their policy holders." Then he added, "We do need churches. There are 11,000 people living in this housing project. There will be 30,000 in this rather compact area. Can you find a better mission field in any suburb, if your churches are really interested in people? My only hope is that the churches that do become established here will stay, come what may. If they do not, it would be far better if they didn't come at all."

A church is not new simply because a congregation was recently organized. New churches are those that witness in depth to their communities; that dare to break the ties of tradition and to develop approaches and methods that meet the mood and temper of their communities; that anticipate change and prepare for change; that help their members recognize God's claim on their lives lest they stray and get lost in the wilderness of materialism and conformity that engulfs them; that raise up within their ranks lay people who articulate their faith in daily life and work; and that stay by their communities through all the changes that come.

There are many recently established congregations that are new in that they do not take the "cafeteria" approach to people; that do not have such low standards as to make possible the cafeteria approach of their members, whereby the offerings are merely laid out for them to choose.

There is, for example, a congregation that was established recently in one of the Rocky Mountain communities. The charter membership included former Mormons, Indian Americans, laborers and management personnel, student and faculty members of a state college. At the first Every Member Visit the sixty members—half of whom had been unchurched—made annual pledges totaling eleven thousand dollars. The congregation is a vital force in the total life of the community.

There are also old churches that are new in that they minister to their todays. A layman said to a planning group, "I have been a charter member of two congregations. They were thrilling experiences. Some months ago I moved into the inner city. I am now a member of an old congregation that through the years has never lost touch with its community. Its membership is in and of the community and is a cross section of its community. It is a redemptive fellowship."

HOME MISSIONS IN LARGER DIMENSIONS

The term "home missions" must take on a broader concept. In common parlance home missions means new church development, financial subsidy to young and small congregations, and special projects such as ministries to Indian Americans, Puerto Ricans, and migrants. In the thinking of most people, home missions, evangelism, social service, and social action are separate departments of the church. In practice there are those who assume that congregations are for those who believe and missions for those who do not. For example, there are many communities that have become blighted and that congregations have abandoned. In the process of relocating, these churches have sought to sell their property to mission boards, claiming that the abandoned communities were naturals for home mission stations. What a tragic story it is that it should be necessary for congregations to move out so that missions might move in.

Mission to the United States and Canada—home missions in its larger dimensions—is the church at work where congregations already exist, reaching out to and ministering to everyone irrespective of nationality, race, or social status. It is the church bearing witness for our Lord Jesus Christ in the rural, urban, and suburban communities alike; it is the loving arm of the church reaching out to Orientals, Negroes, Puerto Ricans, sharecroppers, Jewish people, and all who for one reason or another might be overlooked. It calls for husbanding all resources of men and means and using them as stewards accountable to God.

Several denominations are presently engaged in merger negotiations. How new will these merged communions be?

What creativity and innovation will go into their organizational structures? Are they leaving sufficient openness and flexibility in constitutions so that their structures and polity will be readily adaptable to the rapid changes that are taking place and will continue to take place?

MISSION TERRITORY AGAIN

Urbanization has placed the church in a new missionary situation. "Here," say Walter Kloetzli and Arthur Hillman, "is the world of the elevated, the skyscraper, and the subway; of packing houses, freight yards, docks, steel mills, mail-order houses, universities, television studios, and churches of every creed; of open markets and streets. . . . Here is a world of neon, stone, and steel, and an ever widening household of overflowing millions. Not all have taken the journey to the city, it is true; yet few are removed from the force of its impact and its way of life." [1] The urban dailies, the radio and television stations, the stock exchanges, the stylists, the theater, the magazines, the corporations shape the thinking and behavior of all America.

Can Protestantism develop an urban ministry that recognizes the values of urban life and relates these to witness and obedience to the gospel? Can Protestantism create a program and work out a strategy that will meet the issues of the life of people who live and work and play in the city? Can the church speak prophetically to those who influence the lives of thousands upon thousands? If Protestantism cannot, or will not, then it will have to revise its estimate of the role it wants to play in American life.

Roland Allen has asked what it was that made St. Paul's missionary work so extraordinarily successful. [2] Allen credits

it to "strategic centers." Every major city in which Paul
worked had four distinct features: it was a center of Roman
administration, of Greek civilization, of Jewish influence,
and of world commerce. In other words, Paul's strategy was
built around the centers of government, culture, religion,
and business. His plan was that the gospel should move from
key cities outward until the nation was evangelized. The
prime strategy today, if Scripture is to serve as our guide,
must be in the cities.

While Protestantism has surrendered one citadal after another in the city, the Roman Church continues with aggres-
sive parish programs, endeavors to take changing communities in stride, and works with urban renewal planners. The
Roman Church is not finding it easy, but it does recognize
the strategic position of the city and its growing importance. The strength of the Roman Church has been in the
cities, but with a large Protestant population moving in—
Negroes and whites from the South predominantly—it sees
the cities as missionary territory again. At the same time
the Roman Church is carefully and strategically planting
churches in the suburbs.

The Protestant churches have had their strength in rural
America. The population shift and the emerging new rural
society may be catching them off guard. In the meantime,
the Roman Church is systematically planting one church
after another across rural America.[3] Protestant churches, in
the meantime, carry on their competing ministries in communities and counties—even in communities where population decline is decisive. Larger farms have greatly increased
the size of rural communities, with the result that many
churches are today poorly located.

Dr. Harold E. Fey, editor of *The Christian Century*, said at the Assembly of the Division of Home Missions of the National Council of Churches, in December, 1956, "Protestantism is moving out of the inner city at the time when a predominantly Protestant population has moved in; we are losing our grip on rural life, which has been the seed bed of Protestantism, just when scientific methods, television, and rural electrification have opened a new era in town and country living." The heart of the city and the heart of rural America constitute the basic challenge and opportunity of the church.

Our mission to the suburbs and new communities will become increasingly difficult, our country will become increasingly pagan, and the Protestant churches will become increasingly peripheral unless the churches demonstrate committed and costly concern in these areas and the will to cooperate adventurously. History is full of examples of the outbreak of the Spirit's power in unexpected places and its ability to do the unexpected. The first sign of wisdom is to beware of prophecy—to beware of writing off as hopeless, from the point of view of God's purpose, places where the church appears to have suffered defeat, and to avoid overconfidence about situations where all seems to be well.

THE COMMUNION OF SAINTS

Even the most casual reading of the New Testament makes clear that unity with Christ in his church means vital, costly concern for the total well-being of the family of God. The people of God are mutually responsible before God, one for the other, and for witnessing to their faith in the larger community outside the church.

As members of the Body of Christ, the communion of saints, no one can say to another member, even as no congregation can say to another congregation, "I have no need of you," or "That's your problem. It is no concern or responsibility of mine." We have guidance at this point from Scriptures: "As a matter of equality, your abundance at the present time should supply their want . . . that there may be equality." [4] "If one member suffers, all suffer together." [5]

Fresh breezes are beginning to blow through our churches. We have looked at the graveyards of Protestantism—more than three hundred abandoned churches in Chicago alone—in centers where multitudes are huddled together and where human need and misery cry out to heaven, and we have experienced agony of soul. Our attitudes and behavior have not been those of the communion of saints.

In his annual report a Protestant bishop expressed the growing concern of regional administrators, "We are gradually losing our hold in the city, from which most of the people in the suburbs come and will continue to come. Unless we maintain strength in the city we will not for long be strong in the suburbs either. However, such a consideration looks only to the preservation of the church, not the mission of the church. Our prayers for the people of the inner city must be accompaneid by personnel and money—otherwise we make mockery of prayer. Nor dare we neglect the declining rural communities and kingdom outposts either. Somehow, too, the new communities must be served without neglecting the old parishes in the heart of the city and in the heart of rural America."

Several denominations have conducted special ingatherings and made substantial budget appropriations to provide additional staff and to renovate church buildings in the inner city. In some instances added facilities have been provided.

The various denominations established a $27,000,000 program and challenge to the Protestant community in New York City. This program, called the "Twentieth Century Opportunity," was developed in 1956. Since that time the various denominations co-operating in the program have accepted additional responsibility for more than $16,000,000. These funds are being used for the renovation of existing structures, the establishment of multiple staff and the strengthening of salary scales, the organization of new congregations in needy areas, and the strengthening of all phases of the program of the church.

A recent report of the Division of Urban Work of one board of American missions stated:

. . . various types of aid have been given: 18 congregations have received church extension aid, 25 congregations have benefited from the assignment of special lay workers, 31 congregations have received salary aid, 10 congregations have received urban program grants to their budgets, 17 congregations have been assisted in securing a second pastor, and 2 congregations have received grants as special pilot projects.

One denomination has three or more planning councils in metropolitan areas, made up of pastors and laymen of churches in the city and suburbs. Said one member of such a council, "The church in the city and the church in the suburb are separated by distance, yet are connected by a common heart and purpose. They are 'Siamese twins,' and to separate them may be to sound the death knell of both of them. We turn again to him who said 'Feed my sheep.'

He didn't say where, but he must have meant wherever they are."

It has been suggested that jurisdictional administrators and mission directors confer with pastors of congregations in the city and the suburbs to devise a plan by which "expendable" and "dedicated" and "capable" volunteers can be "loaned" to "struggling and dying" congregations to bolster their morale and serve as lay evangelists, lay teachers, and leadership training people. One pastor whose congregation is involved in such a program, reports, "It has been heartening to observe the spiritual growth in laymen and laywomen giving themselves so completely to this inner city congregation. This is particularly refreshing in light of the fact that this inner city congregation is actually pulling out leadership from men and women who even in their vocational life have had few opportunities to exercise leadership."

Another example of concern in action is that of an established congregation in a metropolitan suburb that is trying to raise $84,000 needed to help a new church in the inner city. This congregation has financial problems of its own: a million dollar plant, mortgaged to the tune of several hundred thousand dollars. "But one of the reasons," says the pastor, "is that we owe existence in part to another church of our denomination, which gave its resources to help us get started thirteen years ago. And we hope that in some way, through this new church, we can repay what the congregation did for us."

A congregation in suburban Chicago is prosecuting a creative ministry in its own changing community and loaning lay leadership to at least two inner city congregations. One inner city congregation refused both financial and leadership assistance from a congregation in a suburb because it was not assuming responsibility for its own changing community.

The Patron Membership Plan has been suggested toward insuring financial security for struggling congregations in city and rural communities. The "patrons" might be former members, as well as others, who would gladly contribute ten, twenty, fifty or more dollars each year (without reducing their financial support to the congregations to which they now belong) to help pay the salary of a parish worker, a social worker, a deaconess, or a youth director. I am acquainted with one social worker in an inner city congregation who is supported by a group of laymen who at one time belonged to that congregation.

There are congregations with endowments that are remitting the major part of interest from these endowments to their judicatories to assist other congregations in the performance of their ministries.[6] Presbyterian congregations in and about Cleveland are giving $1.25 per member toward the support of the Protestant Inner City Parish. Increasingly judicatories and national boards of missions are assisting inner city churches with funds and staff. In not a few instances, long term loans—and sometimes outright gifts—are made available to enable congregations to renovate and modernize their churches.

All such involvements and interactions might well lead to a turning point in urban Protestantism—the upgrading of the ministry of the church in total metropolitan areas. Furthermore, in coming to the rescue of a sister congregation, the stronger rescuing congregation may be led to see the changes taking place in its own community and plan its strategy accordingly. It is a good thing for a church to meet change with change. It is far better for the church to be out in front, leading the way.

The right application of the doctrine of the communion of saints never lends itself to paternalism. Parasitism is the child of paternalism. When a body throws its strength to the rescue of a member, it does so to heal and to strengthen, to the end that the member may function healthily again —to the good of the whole body. Willing and trained lay men and women from other congregations are never used to deprive a local resident or a new convert of opportunity to serve or in any way to retard the development of stewardship of talents and money in the aided congregation. To whatever degree is possible, even in the most transient and insecure congregation, the full utilization of available resources in manpower and money should be emphasized and encouraged. Loaned personnel have done their job effectively when they have worked themselves out of their assignment. The objective is: indigenous congregations— indigenous in terms of membership, leadership, and financial support. It must be understood, however, that in some places it may take a long time before a congregation can become completely indigenous.

CHURCHES FOR THEIR COMMUNITIES

The time has come when Protestantism must take seriously the life that is lived in and through existing congregations. Many congregations are interested in missions. How many recognize that they are themselves missions? For how many is the parish program the connecting link between the congregation and the community? Congregations are commissioned to be apostolic—on mission sent to their respective communities. This remains their ongoing mission, if they are to be the Body of Christ in their communities.

Approximately 95 per cent of the people of our country live within easy reach of existing churches. The losses will be greater than the gains if full attention is not given to the mission of each congregation. A church that recognizes that its best field is in the very community where its congregation is now located is also the church that will be really dynamic in helping plant new missions where they are needed.

The local congregation represents its denomination in its community. Its first witness is to its community. If the congregation does not bear witness, the communion has no witness in that comumnity.

The trouble is that so many Protestant congregations are self-oriented, rather than oriented toward the parishes in which they are located. They have their "clientele" scattered and carry on their evangelism far beyond what should be their parish boundaries. Recently I studied the yearbooks of three congregations of three different communions. The first is in a metropolitan city and has an adult membership of 3,109. Six hundred thirty-five members live within two miles of the church; 573 live outside the two mile boundary but within the city limits; 1,340 live in various suburbs; the remaining 561 live elsewhere in the state or out of the state. The second congregation is in a town of 9,000, and has a membership of 967. Six hundred thirty-one members live in the town or its outskirts; 270 live elsewhere in the state; 66 live out of the state. The third is located in a suburb, and its congregation is seven years old. Of the 421 adult members, 160 live in the suburb in which the church is located;

235 live in seven surrounding suburbs, 26 live in remote communities or out of the state.

Do we really have any right to talk about parish churches unless we have parish church ministries, unless we have front line congregations in the communities where our congregations are located? The local church is related to a particular neighborhood or community. Its primary mission is in that community, whatever the nature of the community. There it is committed to do its primary work.

There are those—pastors and laymen—who counter by saying, "We grant you that it is spiritually harmful for members to be so far removed from their church home that they cannot attend church regularly and cannot participate in the congregation's total life. But your statement goes too far. After all, the parish concept no longer makes sense. Members today live in several communities—their work communities, their social communities, their recreational communities. Many of them live their lives more intimately and more meaningfully in other communities than in those in which they have their residences. Then, too, you forget that the automobile takes people many miles in only a matter of minutes. Why talk about the parish or neighborhood community? It doesn't exist."

Yet, the community or precinct exists when it comes to exercising our voting privilege. And the politician works his precinct, his ward, or his township in full depth. The community or zone exists when it comes to the elementary or high school that our children attend. Why should our children be pulled out of their school and play community to attend church and Sunday school in some distant community once a week? Is church membership a club membership, so we choose the particular club of our denomination that suits our whims or is in keeping with our status? Is it not the business of the local church to break through all the barriers erected by men? Can we not best bear our witness and help build community by sharing in the life of the neighborhood and the neighborhood church? As for our work, social, and recreational communities, are we not Christians at all times and in all places—living out our faith and bearing witness to it in work and play and social life?

There is a strange inconsistency. The denominations have been remiss in not defining parish boundaries. The geographical boundaries of their jurisdictional units and the units within the jurisdictions are carefully defined. Since the churches live through their congregations it would seem important to speak to this matter. The Roman Church has a distinct advantage in this respect. It has parish churches and they serve their parishes.

RELOCATION OF CHURCHES

The question is, should churches relocate at all unless they are relocated in their present communities, in order that they may serve more effectively? It would appear to be far better to plant new churches in the suburbs than to relocate old churches in them. When a congregation no longer has a field in its present community, or is unwilling to serve its changed community, should it not dissolve or merge with another congregation? If there is no field remaining, what is there to relocate? The congregation has served its purpose. If a congregation is unwilling to witness to and serve its changed community—unwilling to give God's gift of grace to all—has it a moral right to relocate?

When a congregation loses its community it is through. There cannot be a congregation without a parish—what happens is that the congregation and the parish have had a divorce, without either of them being conscious of it. When a congregation loses its community it is a good thing to step out and let another congregation do the work of God that it was unwilling or unable to do. We remember what the Master said about the barren fig tree—why should it remain there to cumber the ground? He didn't suggest that it be transplanted.

If a congregation has a decision to make about its future in its community, it would be fortunate for the mission of the church if it had but three choices: 1. to re-tool its program to serve its changed community; 2. to merge with another congregation and thereby strengthen the common witness to that community; 3. to dissolve, allowing time for members to transfer to churches in their respective communities before dissolution becomes effective.

Then, in turn, every new community could have really "new" churches, not bound by the traditions of older congregations.

THE INTERCULTURAL MINISTRY—A TWO-WAY STREET

The intercultural and interracial ministry is a two-way street, with the church enriching the lives of those received into its fellowship and the church, in turn, enriched by their fellowship. It is not absorption or assimilation, but what is aptly called acculturation, the blending of cultures—the two-way process in which each group gives and each receives so much that they are mutually benefited. An integrated congregation is one in which all members share fully and equally in all aspects of church life—from holding office and teaching in the Sunday school to pastoral leadership. There is no second class membership and no second class leadership.

I recall a conversation with a young Estonian DP. I asked him how he was faring in America. He replied, "I have a good job and already have many friends. I belong to a church and sing in the choir. But most of us Estonians feel there is something that isn't right. Our enemies have tried to destroy us, and now our friends try to absorb us. As a people we are destroyed either way. Have we nothing to contribute to the life of a nation?"

A. C. Bouquet reported:

An Oxford-trained African professor who is a citizen of the new state of Ghana has written lately, in effect, that although the member of a social group may wish to drink with others out of a great river, need he use only one sort of cup? He puts forth this challenge as a Christian who is desirous of keeping as much as he reasonably can of his own specific Akan culture. Must Christianity, he asks, change the cup, or cannot it remain content to be the river that fills it? [7]

In the two-way-street ministry the elimination of racial segregation in housing is essential. Open occupancy is necessary if the churches are to be racially inclusive and bring about the reconciliation that must precede an unbroken fellowship. Many of us favor racial desegregation when secondary associations are involved—in school and church and on the job. But we may not be so favorably disposed—and some of us may even be resentful—when we face the prospect of primary associations through residential desegregation. In our parish churches we might well give consideration to such questions as: What is open occupancy? What are the consequences of housing discrimination? What are the housing practices in our community? Shall the wishes of a prejudiced neighbor transcend our Christian responsibility? What are the facts concerning what happens to communities following open occupancy? What are our own attitudes toward open occupancy?

TRAINING FOR CHURCH MEMBERSHIP

Today's mobility challenges the church with the vexing question, "How shall spiritual rootage become a reality in communities and in the lives of people when people do not stay put?" May it not be that the fluidity of population calls for rethinking and reorientation of the church with respect to the meaning of church membership, the scope of church membership, the responsibility to community, and the concern for all people?

The Holy Catholic Church, particularly communions of the non-Roman tradition, has become identified too much with the local congregation. One of the basic weaknesses of the Protestant churches is that their people have not been taught or encouraged to take the church with them wherever they go. Mobility demands a wider vision of the church. Instruction for church membership today calls for emphasis on the primary loyalty to the Church Universal, of which the congregation is the local representation.

This was demonstrated by a young woman, an immigrant from Wales, who belongs to the United Presbyterian Church. Her position has built-in mobility. She is transferred at least twice each year. Asked how she manages to hold life together, she replied, "I have not found it at all difficult.

When I am notified about my next transfer I prepare myself mentally and spiritually for it. When the time comes, I ask my pastor for a transfer to the Presbyterian church in my new community; I notify my bank and tell them I will shortly transfer my account; I pack my belongings and head for my next temporary place of residence. On my arrival I locate a room or small apartment. I bring my letter of transfer to the pastor of the nearby Presbyterian church, and I tell him that my stay in the community will no doubt be of short duration but that I want to take full part in the life of the congregation as long as I am there. I transfer my bank account to the bank of my new community. My life has wider dimensions and I know as never before what it means to belong to the whole church."

A layman was heard to say, "As accurately as I can figure, from the time I was a small lad up to the present, I have belonged to twenty-one congregations. Mobility has been a part of my life. We have made it a policy in our family that wherever we are, we join the closest Lutheran church (at least twice we belonged to a church of another denomination because there was no Lutheran church in the community) and go to work."

There are some real blessings that mobility can bring, rightly understood. A pastor ministers to many more people in a mobile society than in one that is static. Even in declining communities the church is no longer taken for granted. The church that is vital transfers people out when they move to other communities so they will not have to be evangelized all over again—and it meets the newcomer to its own neighborhood with open arms and a mission to accomplish.

Mobility's greatest contribution to the Church of our day is to cause us to re-think and re-shape our basic purposes. Thus, mobility forces us to shift our emphasis from that of building the congregation into a little kingdom, to that of winning people for the Lord Jesus Christ. . . .

This has a double effect on the congregation. First, it makes the congregation more important because it clearly is God's ordained way for reaching people, people who are in the procession. Second, it makes the congregation less important, because it is not an end in itself, but only a means to an end.[8]

NEW MISSION DEVELOPMENT

The goal of church extension is not to reproduce a human institution, properly incorporated, founded on constitution and bylaws, but that a divine institution shall come into being, founded on Word and Sacraments, a creation of the Holy Spirit. When mission is equated with reproducing identical units it degenerates into propaganda. The same is true when church extension means getting there first—particularly to the "productive" fields—with a denominational program. It smacks of the world and not of the gospel in motivation.

The occupancy of a field should be predicated on both need and opportunity. There are high potential fields that give quick return to the missionary dollars and the missionaries' ministries. There are fields of normal potential. Such communities cannot be by-passed. There are the low potential fields—low in terms of economic status but high in terms of people. Here, there is real danger that, like the priest and Levite, the churches may pass by on the other side or salve their consciences by establishing a few token congregations.

American mission strategy calls for that kind of over-all planning that involves the various types of fields, without selfishly motivated preferment, in unchurched or under-churched inner cities, older city neighborhoods, high rise apartment communities, smaller cities, suburban and exurban communities, military communities, trailer parks, retirement centers, mushrooming communities of migrant people who are establishing home bases, strip cities.

On the one hand, all denominational boards of missions and jurisdictional units need to develop their respective over-all strategies, which will embrace the various kinds of communities. But if America is to be churched responsibly there is need of co-operative planning on the part of all Protestant bodies. Planning principles and procedures must be hammered out that will be a guide for establishing only those congregations that will have maximum opportunity for effective life and work. (See Chapter 6.)

FINANCING NEW MISSION CHURCHES

The commitment of a board of missions or jurisdictional unit to establish a congregation in any community carries with it the commitment to provide necessary loans for pur-chase of site, construction of the first unit of the church complex, and usually for the down payment on the pastor's residence. Both the cost of sites—averaging about three acres —and the cost of construction continue to increase. Church extension fund administrators report that the cost of sites averages $25,000 and the cost of constructing and furnishing a first unit averages $60,000. To be sure, there are projects that total only $40,000, but a few have exceeded $200,000.

No denomination has church extension funds adequate to

house the congregations that have been established. Some boards of missions encourage congregations, wherever possible, to use rented quarters until at least a specified percentage of cost of building and site have been received. There are other boards that purchase the site, build a first unit, and secure the residence for the pastor before further work is initiated. In any event, congregations are being housed and congregations continue to be established. How is this made possible?

1. A number of mission boards have induced church colleges, seminaries, and other church-related institutions to make substantial loans to new mission congregations from their endowments and other investment funds. All loans are set up on monthly amortization schedules. For the protection of the investors the boards of missions guarantee the monthly repayments. It would seem that many church institutions would be eager to loan funds in this way for church expansion. In pleading for church extension investments in renewal areas Meryl Ruoss has raised a moral question about investment portfolios of church institutions:

A recent study I did in one denomination alone showed that 280 million had been invested by their national boards in some enterprise or other. I didn't investigate the actual portfolios but if some denominations I know are typical a sizable proportion of those funds were invested in things like General Motors and Standard Oil. . . . We build guns and tanks and planes and bombs with our church investments. Here is one of the great opportunities for life-*saving* investment. Let us enter *in* to the urban renewal program with our vast invested sums.[9]

2. The Mission Builder program is another approach. Debt free congregations, and congregations with

debts that are insignificant in comparison with the worth of their properties, have mortgaged their buildings in order to make loans to new missions. Here again, the boards of missions guarantee the monthly repayments, and it is reported that there has not been a single default to date. In one denomination such loans total more than four million dollars. This denomination reports further that several congregations are Mission Builders for the second and third time.

3. Something similar to Savings and Loan Associations have been established by some denominations. They are called by various names, such as God's Bank, Mission Development Certificate Plan, Trust Certificate Plan. This is a way whereby members' savings can do double duty—increase the loan funds for church extension and provide earning as well as security on investments. The plan is simple. Certificates in denominations of $50, $100, $500, $1,000, and $5,000 are sold to individuals, congregations, institutions, and agencies. The interest paid is on the modest side, 4 per cent by one denomination. The church extension administrator of one denomination reports that $39,850,000 in such investments have been sold.

4. There is the Mission Sponsor Plan that has been adopted by at least two denominations. Individuals commit themselves to contribute $10, $25, or $100 toward the purchase of a site for a congregation that has been established within the jurisdictional area in which they have their membership.

5. A number of new congregations have set up their own debenture bond programs and have sold enough bonds to their members and members of other churches to finance their first unit. In one synod a number of churches banded

together to form an association to sell such bonds in order to make loan funds available for new congregations.

6. It was common practice until recently for boards of missions to set up amortization schedules on a ten or fifteen year repayment plan. Administrators have discovered that by reducing the repayment period to five years they have doubled or tripled the worth of their capital funds and strengthened their borrowing capacity. In high and normal potential communities this is regular procedure in a growing number of denominations. In order to accomplish this, attention is given to a strong stewardship program in the local congregation at the outset. A fund appeal is conducted no later than the third year of the congregation's life. By the time the congregation is five years old, it has sufficient equity in its property to secure its own mortgage for the balance of the indebtedness. One board has reduced the repayment schedule to three years.

7. Members of at least three recently established congregations have made arrangements to increase their personal home mortgages, and thereby are able to make substantial loans to their church building funds. In one instance these contributions totalled $58,000.

The story is told of a young couple very much in love. One evening, as they were sitting together on a hillside overlooking a moonlit lake, he said, "Mary, if you could be anything you wanted to be, what would it be?" Mary looked at him and said, "John, I would just want to be a rosebud in the lapel of your coat, resting on your shoulder, and looking up at your strong, handsome face." Then she asked, "And John, what would you like to be?" He turned to Mary and said, "I would like to be an octopus so I could enfold you with all eight of my arms." "John, you cannot mean what you are saying," she retorted. "You aren't even using the two you have." Here we have the answer to marshalling both our financial and human resources. The resources are in our parish churches. The question is, "To what extent are the resources being made available?"

LEADERSHIP FOR THE CHURCHES

According to the New Testament, the ministry is a general concept and includes a variety of services. The ministry is the prerogative and responsibility of the whole Body of Christ. This responsibility is exercised by the members of the household of faith in a ministry to one another as individuals and in voluntary services to the entire fellowship. The responsibility is also exercised by action of the household of faith in delegating responsibility to certain persons to perform assignments or offices on behalf of an entire denomination, its regional units, or the congregation.

It is an encouraging sign that the churches, on all levels, are employing more and more laymen and laywomen to serve professionally in various capacities. Hundreds of pastors were until recently—and many still are—employed in occupations that are at best only indirectly related to their special function. In practically every denomination lay people have replaced ministers as presidents of colleges; superintendents of hospitals, children's homes, and homes for the aged; directors of social service, stewardship education, and pension funds; and many other administrative positions.

This is true on the congregational level as well. Business administrators, parish workers, directors of religious education, youth directors, ministers of music, social service workers, an assortment of secretaries and other full time and part time workers are providing leadership and services that increase the effectiveness of the parish churches. And they are reducing substantially what Joseph Sittler of the Federated Faculty of the University of Chicago calls "the masc eration of the minister." [10] Many smaller congregations employ part time workers. In some communities several churches combine resources to employ competent personnel.

The net result is not only more efficiency—and should not the church be efficient in the discharge of its total steward ship?—but there has developed a team ministry of pastors and laity that is all to the good and a harbinger of better things to come. The lay people in the employment of the church are bridging the gap between the clergy and the laity. There is less and less clericalism. Thank God for that!

Shortage Of Pastors

As Protestants we will need ". . . to establish three thousand churches every year in the foreseeable future, just to keep pace with the increase of population, not taking into account the need to gain the unchurched" according to H. Conrad Hoyer.[11]

On this basis, population increase alone calls for thirty thousand more Protestant congregations during this decade.

Additional clergy are needed as missionaries abroad, seminary professors, institutional chaplains, college and university pastors, assistant ministers in large congregations, and in other areas.

The present enrollment in theological seminaries does not meet the needs of the immediate future, let alone provide for accelerated demands for pastoral leadership. Parenthetically, it should be noted that the shortage of parish priests in the Roman Church is fully as critical.

There are many reasons for this shortage, but the important question is, "How shall the churches secure the ministers that are needed?"

Changing Times reports that ". . . all of the churches are concentrating on highly selective recruitment programs, including psychological testing, to seek out young men who are suited to the religious vocation and will stay in it." [12] Such efforts center in national and regional Men for the Ministry conferences. Recently one denomination conducted ninety one-day area conferences for young men, attended by three thousand youth, eight hundred ministers, and a like number of laymen.

Theological seminaries have held conferences on the ministry, usually week-long sessions attended by college students. Out of three such conferences at one interdenominational seminary, 75 per cent of the men in attendance enrolled after graduation in a theological school.

Some churches are working with seminaries in adjusting requirements to make it possible for middle-aged men to enter the ministry. A surprising number of men are turning to this field after successful careers in business or professions.

Stephen Neill has asked:

Are we not once again driven towards the conclusion that each of these centres should have its own minister . . . drawn from the neighbourhood and from those who earn their living in lay avocations? [Dr. Neill here refers to small congregations without a pastor, or several congregations served by a single pastor.] Dare we go further, and venture to affirm that, if the local fellowship, still related to the large Church for common acts of worship, is to centre locally, as it ought to do, on the Table of the Lord, all these local ministers should receive such ordination as would enable them to minister †.e Lord's Supper in their neighbourhood and for the people of their fellowship? . . . Undoubtedly there would be difficulties; but these difficulties ought not to stand in the way of courageous experiment on a large scale and in many directions. . . . Everything to-day suggests that the risks involved in experiment are less than those of trying to maintain inflexibly the traditions that have come down from the past.[13]

Shortage Of Other Professionals

Not only is there shortage of pastors but also of laymen and laywomen in the employment of the church. In every area of salaried service the shortage is critical. Practically all denominations have created recruitment offices. Counselors from such recruitment offices "make their pitch" at summer Bible camps, on college campuses (particularly during Religious Emphasis Week), youth retreats, and conferences.

Let it be remembered, however, that men and women for the various ministries of the church grow up in our parish congregations. In the final analysis it is to the congregations that the denominations must turn. The pastors and other church staff personnel, as well as men and women for all vocations, are in our Sunday schools and youth groups, at worship in our parish churches, and in our parish homes today.

There are many natural opportunities to keep the need for pastors and other staff workers in the church before the people of our congregations: in the corporate prayer of the congregation at worship, "Pray therefore the Lord of the harvest to send out laborers into his harvest" [14]; in sermons, Bible studies, Sunday school; in confirmation classes or other pastor's classes, including the private conferences; in youth group discussions on vocation; in opening the way for children and youth to serve in the congregation, which includes assisting the pastor at the altar; in confronting parents with their opportunity and responsibility to guide their children into their life's vocation.

It is to full time and full life service that all Christians are called regardless of place or area of service. Men and women who are looking for adventure need not—at least in our day —pass by the Christian cause. There is plenty of adventure, and there are crosses waiting and ready to be given out to Christians who are ready for them and who are unwilling to let their religion be cozy and comfortable. The demand is for Christians who will dare to lift the Cross above the customs and standards of the present world—dare to attack the strongholds of economic and social paganism, the class prejudices and race bigotries—and lift up their voices to him who is Truth and Life.

6:

CHURCHING

AMERICA RESPONSIBLY

The Christian cause thrives and makes its greatest impact when its followers, as servants of Christ, are hard at work carrying on the Master's work in his spirit.

St. Paul was greatly distressed by the individualism and divisiveness of the congregation in Corinth. In his first letter, after stating his concern, he became specific: "What I mean is that each one of you says, 'I belong to Paul,' or 'I belong to Apollos,' or 'I belong to Cephas,' or 'I belong to Christ.' Is Christ divided?" [1] Then he proceeded to show how foolish and hurtful this dissension was and set forth the servant role of the church and of every member. He held before the Corinthians a basic fact, "For we are fellow workmen for God." [2] And in his anxiety over the unity as well as the expansion of the church, Paul pleaded with the members of the church in Ephesus to "Accept life with humility and patience, making allowances for each other because you love each other. Make it your aim to be at one in the Spirit, and you will inevitably be at peace with one another. You all belong to one Body, of which there is one Spirit, just as you all experienced one calling to one hope." [3]

Individuals merge into the common good of the church of Christ and lend united strength to the task of the ongoing mission that will remain unfinished until the kingdoms of this world become Christ's kingdom. What is true of the individual Christian is true of the individual congregation and the individual denomination. We are workmen together *for God!*

The fact that we ". . . are the body of Christ and individually members of it" [4] and that we ". . . are his workmanship, created in Christ Jesus for good works" [5] must take on fresh relevance if we are to church America responsibly in these days of rapid change.

The population explosion, the emerging megalopolis, large scale home construction, urban redevelopment, mass mobility and population shift, and the agricultural revolution challenge the churches to new adventures in planning and working together creatively. New churches, new service to people, adjustment in local patterns, the development of priorities, and the effective deployment of resources give ample evidence of the need for responsible and cooperative strategy. This is a time of crucial decisions for the survival and effectiveness of individual congregations and for the determination of the shape and content of the Protestant witness.

John D. Lange is concerned because: "Many new neighborhoods are now being planned, unfortunately without regard to direct church needs, and I think principally it's up to the churchmen to reflect their views and make their direct interests known to the officials. I don't believe it's an intentional oversight but one in which the official bodydom in the communities needs terrific amounts of guidance and

I think church people can offer that guidance on quite a substantial scale." [6]

Dr. Reid Ross of the Cincinnati Better Housing League, in a nine point program, makes a plea that the churches exercise spiritual and moral leadership so that there may be some compassionate understanding of the deep and troublesome human problems emerging from the process of city rebuilding.[7]

Those who plan and shape the city of tomorrow face difficult problems that must concern the churches. Walter Kloetzli, director of Urban Church Planning of the National Lutheran Council, has asked:

Shall families in blighted areas be permitted to "double up"— perhaps three families share the living space normally required for one? Shall speculative home builders be devoid of responsibility for schools and playgrounds in mushrooming suburbs— yes and for providing church sites? Whose responsibility are the dispossessed—those persons made homeless by re-development projects? Shall the four-wheeled altar of modern man, the automobile, so dominate that the expressways and throughways always be given top priority—at the expense of parks and other equally important non-essentials? At what stage of neighborhood decline and deterioration does one become concerned about conservation? Shall new and renewed neighborhoods or housing projects be homogenous—or shall they be non-segregated as to class, age, race? [8]

Studies show that non-farm areas extending beyond the suburbs are largely unchurched. Are these unchurched people to be reached through existing congregations? Are additional congregations required? Will these areas become overchurched or overlooked?

Decisions must also be made by congregations in rural communities. On the one hand, there are rural areas that are unchurched and underchurched. On the other hand, thousands of rural communities, particularly declining communities, are overchurched. Perhaps all of us can agree that if the Protestant witness is to be maintained in rural America, it must be strengthened. If this can be done by having two congregations rather than three, or four instead of two, we must move in whichever direction can bring the greater effectiveness. This involves the give and take of planning.

CASES IN POINT

1. Here is an inner city neighborhood. Presently there are six large Protestant churches and one Roman Catholic church in the area. All six Protestant churches are in a bad way. Their memberships are scattered. Their buildings are deteriorating. Each congregation is carrying on its program with little hope for survival. Three or possibly four churches in this neighborhood, properly staffed and programmed, could carry on effective ministries.

2. Here is a suburban community, in a three-square-miles area, with a population of 7,400. There are presently eight Protestant churches and three more under construction. Four of them are on the same street, less than two blocks apart. This denominational competition, and the desire of all church bodies to be represented in each major housing area, actually bewilders both the subdivision developer and the suburban dwellers.

3. Here is a declining rural community. Population has dwindled from 2,400 to 2,000. The seven Protestant churches are struggling to keep alive. All of them are parts

of two and three congregation parishes. Two of the congregations have been without pastoral leadership for more than a year. Neither on the jurisdictional nor local level is there any conversation going on that might lead to a decision as to how many and which of the congregations shall continue.

4. And here is an open country area six miles square with six Protestant churches. The country school and the general store have closed. Announcement has been made that three of the congregations will dissolve within the next few months. If one or more of them should disband, should not the jurisdictional leaders of the denominations represented in the other churches be advised? Should not provision be made for the spiritual care of the few remaining members of the dissolving congregation?

5. Here is a large tract where a developer expects to build 1,300 homes. He consults with political and school authorities. What about the church? He has no problem with the Roman Catholic Church. But the Protestant churches do present problems, for eighteen denominations have asked to purchase three to five acre sites. The developer will make three sites available when they have agreed which three should establish congregations.

REGIONAL AND LOCAL CO-OPERATION

The Division of Home Missions of the National Council of Churches in February, 1957, made a study of polity and practice in new church development. Fourteen denominations participated. The report of the study reads in part:

While there is a wide variety of distribution of authority and there are discrepancies between theory and practice, there seem to be clear indications of a clustering of real power and crucial decision making at the regional level, often rather narrowly defined—the state, the metropolitan area, the diocese, the synod, the district.[9]

The report of the study indicates rather sharply that the strategy and decisions involved in establishing congregations are largely at the regional level. Failure to develop a rational series of premises for co-operative planning can only result in repeating the story of duplication, increasingly competitive loyalties, and serious gaps in the Christian ministry. If resources are to be used wisely, a comprehensive picture of needs and opportunities must be made available, since it is not possible for one denomination to plan well if it is ignorant of the plans of sister communions. Even the person who is most loyal to his particular tradition knows there cannot possibly be a church of his communion in every community. He knows, too, that churching America responsibly is a job that cannot be done by a single denomination.

It is important also to recognize that the problem of over-churching in a neighborhood or community will never be solved without involvement of the jurisdictional administrators. By the same token, regional involvement will never be effective without involvement and decision making on the congregational level. It is "both-and"—not "either-or." Studies, dialogue, decision making must be co-operative.

SOME ENCOURAGING ROAD SIGNS

1. The climate for planning in co-operation with community agencies is favorable. Milton Breivogal, director of planning, county of Los Angeles, said, "We believe the information we have in our office of the population, its dis-

tribution, composition, and characteristics, and the periodi-
cal estimates we are making by geographical areas can be
very helpful to the church planner. My planning department
is ready to help make available our resources." This, we
believe, is typical of the attitude of most community planning directors, many of whom are active members of
churches. Their wealth of information and experience, as
well as their concepts of planning, can serve the churches to
excellent advantage. At the same time these directors thereby
become familiar with the concerns of the churches.

2. In several cities—Indianapolis, New York, Detroit, Los Angeles, and others—departments of church planning are in operation and their contributions are significant.
Regional administrators and local leaders (both pastors and
laymen) are satisfied that some real progress has been made
in their strategy studies and common planning. One pastor
commented, "To be sure there has been tension, but it has
been fruitful tension."

3. Co-operative undertakings among and between
the churches include such projects as work among migrants
and Indian Americans, services of worship in national parks,
the World Day of Prayer, the annual study materials on
home and world missions with themes agreed upon interde-
nominationally through the Commission on Missionary Education, institutes and conferences sponsored by the divisions
and departments of the National Council of Churches and
other interdenominational groups, radio and television programs produced by groups pooling their resources and
working together.

4. We have a body of experience in working together on the local level. This includes conducting religious

census, supporting released time classes related to schools, agreeing on church nights on school calendars, addressing ourselves to issues of moral and social concern, working with community organizations, co-operating in programs for mass communications media. There are also thrilling stories of mergers and realignments. There are co-operative ministries —the West Side Parish of Chicago, the East Harlem Protestant Parish, the Protestant Parish of Cleveland, and others. There are also the larger parish experiments in rural communities.

5. Churches of different traditions which have hitherto had little to do with one another—except in heated controversy—have been learning that they share together a common life in Christ. This does not mean minimizing differences in the essentials of the faith; in some respects these have been accentuated through closer contact and freer interchange of views. But the groups involved have learned from one another and are discovering that regardless of their traditions they are expressions of the Church Universal in their communities.

CHURCH PLANNING CONCEPTS

While the term "comity" is by definition acceptable, it has fallen into disfavor in many church bodies because it has come to connote legislation and authoritarianism. The expression "co-operative planning" has, as a result, come into common usage and has acceptance in all parts of the country and in practically all church circles, on national, regional, and local levels. It has the advantage of being understood by planners in other areas of activity and by Mr. Average Citizen.

"Comity" came to mean "contract," and this several denominations would not accept. "Co-operative planning" is voluntary agreement based on common concern and good will. Leland Gartrell, executive secretary of Church Planning and Research of the Protestant Council of the City of New York, has said: "The resources, the traditions, the decision making processes that most profoundly affect the life of the Protestant community lie in the denominational life and work. It is our responsibility to respect these premises and so conduct ourselves that we may be an asset rather than a liability to the total Protestant community. Legislative or authoritarian approaches to denominations break down communications and hinder (at times destroy) the planning process."

The by-laws of the Division of Research and Planning of the Church Federation of Indianapolis state as the purpose of the division: "To endeavor to assist all denominations in securing adequate opportunities to minister to the people of the Metropolitan Indianapolis area and to provide a well-rounded Christian ministry to the entire population. It seeks to insure that no community is either overchurched or left without adequate ministry."

As a general principle it can be said that church planning has as its purpose to develop comprehensive plans, *based on competent and careful research,* through which, according to agreed-upon procedures, the churches, separately and together, may best serve the people of communities involved.

John Halko, secretary-director of the Department of Research and Planning of the Greater Philadelphia Council of Churches, calls attention to what he believes are four essentials in the co-operative church planning process:

1. *Time* is required to educate and establish mutual confidence in areas where co-operation has not existed. (*Author's comment:* This applies also to working with denominations that have not been related to comity committees.)

2. *Patience* is necessary to endure misunderstandings and allow time for massed inertia to change and to move.

3. *Leadership* should be tactful and sensitive.

4. There should be a *sense of awareness* that the work of the Father will be forwarded by co-operation, and all should be aware that each co-operator will be strengthened.

Mr. Halko suggests that there are problems in the planning process, and here he speaks from experience. This should not surprise us. We are familiar with problems in the planning process between boards in our denominations. We know that planning in our congregations has headaches and heartaches. But the problems are slight compared with those that will develop unless we learn to plan co-operatively.

A FIVE-FOLD PROPOSAL

In view of the favorable climate for co-operation, the commonly recognized need, the stewardship of resources, and the generally acceptable church planning concepts, Walter Kloetzli has set forth the following five proposals:

1. Recognize that fundamental facts concerning growth and adjustment are not matters of doctrine, and therefore that Protestants can actively participate together in securing these facts and can share in budgets and directing active research.

2. Co-operate in determining Protestant needs in relation to urban growth and adjustment, and co-operate in presenting these needs to city and community planners and to housing developers.

3. Develop a formula for determining the need for the respective denominational churches in relation to the need and responsibility for other Protestant churches so that the most effective total Protestant witness can be achieved.

4. Recognize that there are significant doctrinal differences between Protestants and plan within the Protestant whole so that the total witness may be represented in each section of the urban area, including the expanding suburbs.

5. Establish a structure for Protestant planning and adjustment through which all plans for new congregations, radical program changes in established churches, and church withdrawals from established fields will be cleared. The structure should be consultative and advisory rather than regulatory. It should be responsible for establishing norms for adequate churching and interpreting the spiritual wisdom of these norms to the denominations. It should recommend to the denominations strategic adjustments that ought to be made in the light of urban growth and change.

A CHURCH PLANNING STRUCTURE

The question uppermost in the minds of many is what kind of structure can be developed, without compromise of principle, that can carry a full share of responsibility. There can be no effective co-operative church planning unless we have confidence in one another and respect one another's principles, with all their theological implications.

Dr. H. Conrad Hoyer, associate executive secretary for Co-operative Planning of the Division of Home Missions of the National Council of Churches, gives helpful clarification at this point:

The structure must provide adequate information, and the means for thinking and planning together, without, however,

giving the structure the authority to regulate by commanding
or forbidding what the co-operating churches shall finally do
except insofar as Christian conscience or good judgment determine. . . .

Admittedly there are theological implications as well as ethical
ones. Surely, one implication is that churches of a given denomination are a part of the "Body of Christ" and as such they should
seek to do their responsible share as a part of the whole. A
second corollary implication is that the "Body of Christ" includes more than churches of one denomination. Planning at
this level assumes that other denominations also witness to the
truth of the Gospel and offer God's Redeeming Grace, so that
they can serve responsibly in His name where we are not now
serving or do not plan to serve. . . . If we recognize that in
spite of our differences we share responsibility with other denominations in the proclamation of the Gospel, then our stewardship responsibility for this Gospel proclamation requires that
we plan as wisely and as well as we can, that it be proclaimed
as widely as possible.[10]

Denominational representatives who are not able to accept
these corollaries will either have to assume responsibility for
maintaining or establishing congregations of their persuasion
in every community in America or live under the agonizing
burden of believing that those communities not ministered
to by them are outside the fellowship of God's grace.

It would seem that a structure for church planning should
provide for:

　　　1. Adequate corporate research and means of communication to persons and groups concerned.

　　　2. A forum to provide opportunities to discuss
norms for Protestant church needs, and to hear denominations express their interest in developing or changing areas.

3. An instrument for regular hearings on plans for church extension, plans for withdrawal of churches, and plans for radical program change.

Perhaps no one person has given more thought to or has had more experience in co-operative church planning than Meryl Ruoss. As one who is familiar with the power structure of the several denominations and is a pioneer in the planning process, he has developed a concept of the principles and structure of co-operative planning that has met with general acceptance. Conceptually and practically it is overarching in that it comprehends the planning process of both regional and local levels.

It is ardently hoped that many regional administrators, pastors, lay leaders, and others who read this chapter have had an opportunity to read carefully his paper, "Toward a Definition of Church Planning." Space permits the barest summary of his text:

1. Church planning is a title applied to the co-operative planning process at the regional level. It focuses on the region— the metropolitan area, the state, the urban region. a. *Authority* —this is a delegation from the appropriate denominational jurisdiction. b. *Continuity*—there must be a serious commitment to the planning process by the decision-making bodies in order to achieve direction, fruitful feedback, and long term effect on policy. c. *Diversity*—a church planning program should produce a Protestant co-operative plan as well as a plan for each denomination. d. *Resources*—to provide the competent staff and the necessary information for a church planning program requires sustained financial support. Staff interprets research and maintains working relationships with civic planners and community developers.

2. A church planning program will produce a regional policies plan for the implementation of the mission of the church, setting forth its specific dimensions, the resources needed, and the time span of action. It will provide for evaluation of experience and encourage congregations and individual church members to understand the scope of the mission. Such understanding is essential if denominations are to develop an adequate strategy for the years ahead.

3. Advising is another function of a church planning process. This helps the denomination to define its goals and priorities in the light of the total responsibility. A proper church planning process emphasizes intelligent choices on the part of denominations but is not an abridgment of the freedom of choice—even the freedom to be wrong. Congregations, too, have that freedom.

4. The church planning process also serves a co-ordinating function, relating decisions to time schedules, resources to priorities, a specific unit to the whole, the church to the city or region, and short term decisions to long term goals and policies.

EFFECTIVE CHURCH PLANNING

If the planning process on the regional level is to be effective it must involve the home mission divisions, the jurisdictional units, and the local congregations. Each can find its place in helping to form the front line of the mission rather than as an autonomous unit. All must have a part. Except as adequate planning exists at all these levels, there is real danger that the process will break down at one point or another.

Churching America in co-operative responsibility is not a partnership of mutual convenience. It is a partnership in obedience to the command of Christ to preach the gospel to *everyone.* If this obedience is lacking, the partnership lacks that which structure cannot give. Above all, there is need for the Christian communions to pray for one another and permit the Holy Spirit to create and strengthen bonds of understanding and concern to the end that they will be led into a fuller realization of their oneness in the Body of Christ.

7:

THE CHURCH'S
FRONT LINE

When we speak of the whole church of Christ on earth, we remember that this church is made up of congregations. What the church does or fails to do depends upon what is happening in and through the congregations.

We address ourselves in this chapter to the church in its local manifestation—to the church as it makes impact, or fails to make impact, on Mr. Average Citizen. The congregation cannot decide whether or not it will effect the life in its community. It does so by its very existence: by its physical presence; by its worship, teaching, action; and by the everyday life and activity of its members. It is the front line, the cutting edge against the world. If it is to minister, and not to be ministered to, it must take the form of a servant, ". . . always carrying in the body the death of Jesus, so that the life of Jesus may also be manifested in our bodies." [1]

Since the local congregation is the visible representation of the whole church in its community, it, too, must be catholic and apostolic. A non-Roman congregation, if it rightly understands its nature, has greater possibility of being catholic and apostolic than does a Roman Catholic congregation.

It has the dimension of being evangelical as well as catholic and apostolic.

However, this catholicity and apostolicity are but wishful thinking unless the congregation is the church—not an institution but a life, not an organization primarily but an organism. When we speak of the Church as Christ's Body, this applies to the local church as well as to the whole church. "Now you are the body of Christ and individually members of it" [2]—inside and outside the parish church.

The discovery of the congregation as the church is of first importance today. Only insofar as the congregation "comes to itself" will it sense its peculiar mission as well as its organic relationship to the Universal Church. Such realization is what Jeroslav Pelikan terms "identification" and "universality." While the congregation is the organ through which Christ himself is at work in a particular community, it shares the fellowship and responsibility of the Universal Church. The call of the church for service and support, in home and world missions, in the ministry of mercy, in Christian education, or in any phase of its world-wide mission is not a call from the outside, as many would argue in defense of non-support or meager support, but is the call of the very Lord himself from within.

The primitive church ". . . devoted themselves to the apostles' teaching and fellowship, to the breaking of bread and the prayers." [3] A congregation that observes these practices is catholic and apostolic, and has no other choice than to be the functioning, living Body of Christ. Because the first Christians were devoted to the apostolic teaching and fellowships, to the prayers, and to the Sacrament, they knew the real meaning of oneness—oneness with God through

Jesus Christ and oneness with each other through Jesus Christ. "And all who believed were together and had all things in common." [4] They distributed help as anyone had need, they attended the temple, they supported one another in prayer, they took their food with glad hearts and praised God. And the result? "And the Lord added to their number day by day those who were being saved." [5]

The early Christians were what God intended the whole church and every congregation to be—a divine society and a missionary fellowship. Again and again in his letters to the churches St. Paul reminded them that the congregation was the Body of Christ and each member individually a part of the body. To live by the reality of this truth is to be a catholic congregation.

There is a church in Minneapolis that bears the name of Good Shepherd. Above the altar there is a bronze silhouette of the head of Christ, fastened to the brick wall. Below and to the left—as one faces the altar—is a shepherd's staff. The symbol reminds the congregation of its catholicity and apostolicity. Christ, the Good Shepherd who gave his life for the sheep on the altar of the Cross, is the head of the congregation. It is significant and telling that only the silhouette of the head is portrayed. The congregation is his body —his voice, eyes, ears, feet, hands, his diverse gifts. In order for Christ to be known in the world there must be mouths that proclaim the word, eyes that see, ears that hear, feet that travel across the street and across the world, hands that bind up the world's wounds. Everyone has a job to do. The failure of any member to do his job weakens the whole body's effectiveness. Thank God, there is also the shepherd's staff! As Christ's own go out into their world, he goes before them. Wherever they are, wherever they go, whatever they do, they belong to him. Come what may, they are safe: ". . . no one is able to snatch them out of the Father's hand." [6] They come into daily contact with sheep who are not of his fold. Through them his voice is heard and others are added to the sheepfold. "So there shall be one flock, one shepherd." [7]

THE WORSHIPING COMMUNITY

Since the church's catholicity consists in the universality of Christ's redeeming work, and since Christ is redemptively at work wherever the gospel is proclaimed, the church has no more catholic expression on earth than in the worship of the local congregation. It is in the local gathering of believers that we join ". . . with angels and archangels and with all the company of heaven," and with the whole church on earth, in praising God's glorious name.

There is a considerable difference in the ordering of worship among the various non-Roman churches. However, we are as one in acknowledging that the saving knowledge of God through Jesus Christ is the most precious possession we have on earth and that it is of the essence to keep that knowledge alive through the fellowship of worship. Before all else, the Christian community is a fellowship united by worship of the God and Father of our Lord Jesus Christ. That is the essential bond of unity. A congregation that does not meet primarily for worship to acknowledge God's gift of salvation and sustaining grace is not a church at all. It has no Godward dimensions. Worship is the congregation's celebration of the presence of God. God is in the midst of the congregation when his people gather to hear the word preached and receive the sacrament.

Most of the activities of the church are shared or can be shared by other institutions, groups, and agencies. The unique privilege and responsibility of the church is to keep open a house of worship, bid men to worship, and seek earnestly to make the worship vital and meaningful to all. To that end people are gathered as congregations and to that end we build churches. If the church loses faith in worship, becomes careless about worship or unconcerned about the fellowship of worship, it need not look to its many varied activities to save it. It is dead at the heart. It has lost its Godward direction.

The early Christians knew poverty and hindrance, but nothing could keep them from coming together for worship. They encouraged one another, ". . . not neglecting to meet together." [8] Worship was a must! When persecutions came and they could no longer worship in their accustomed places, they met in caves and catacombs. There they worshiped. The oldest and most meaningful symbols of the church come to us from those Christian comrades who made caves and catacombs their temples.

As we worship in our parish churches at specific times, we know that the worship, strictly speaking, does not begin nor end at a particular hour. The worship of the church never ceases and when formal worship begins, a congregation in any given place is simply entering into the praise that never ceases.

The corporate worship of the congregation is the godly expression of the whole Body of Christ. The private devotions of individual Christians, the family worship of the

Christian home, and the prayer-meeting are dependent on
the corporate worship of the people of God. Scriptures
make it clear that the mission of the church proceeds from
the center outward rather than from the circumference inward. The nave and the chancel interdepend. Each member
is incorporated into the fellowship of those who receive and
respond to God's love and who discover they are fighting
the same battles. All are sinners who live on forgiveness. A
story is told of an army colonel who worshiped in a parish
church with his regiment. When the time came to receive
Holy Communion the colonel went forward but his men did
not deem it proper to go forward with him. The colonel
turned to them and said, "Out on the field I am your colonel
and I give orders, but at the Lord's table we are all of the
same rank."

Each church member comes expectantly to the house of
God for cleansing, feeding, restoration, renewal. Here all
are one and all have the same basic needs. A young man
said to his pastor as he left church one Sunday morning,
"Now I feel clean and new and whole." He knew why he
went to church and what it meant to worship. He didn't
merely saunter in, saunter through, saunter out, and then
say he had worshiped. I remember an electrical engineer
in a parish I was once privileged to serve who said to me,
"Pastor, I wouldn't be able to live without the church. Out
in the world I get dirty and hungry and tired. While I am
grateful that the church is open every day so I can stop in
for a moment or two, by Friday I can hardly wait for
Sunday to come so that I can gather with the congregation
for worship." Such people say with the Psalmist, "I was
glad when they said to me, let us go to the house of the

Lord." [9] And with the publican of the parable they cry out, "God, be merciful to me a sinner." [10] Regardless of season or weather, such people are never absent from the house of God. They experience God's presence in Word and Sacrament in the fellowship of the congregation.

Someone has said that to the angels a congregation that gathers for worship must look like a shore tide in late afternoon. The shore is littered with all kinds of debris. Then the tide comes in and the water gathers all the debris it can reach and pulls it back into the ocean. The shore is clean once again. So it is that God comes with his tide of grace and buries all the sins of his erring, penitent children in the ocean of his love.

One additional comment on the congregation at worship: The offertory needs to be recovered in its deep meaning. This means that we must, in gratitude and faith, present our sacrificial money offerings not only to support the work of God's church at home and abroad, but also as a symbol of our work and vocation, our brain and brawn and skill—all surrendered to him in disciplined and glad service. In the Prayer of Intercession we lift our homes and work and community to the throne of grace. We pray for all sorts and conditions of men, for all useful arts and sciences, and all fruitful harvests—presenting these for the purpose of God who created them. Our personal prayers are joined with the prayers of the whole church. In prayer and service we are never alone. The praying church supports the servant charged with the proclamation and listens to what God wills to say through him as a word from God and not from men. In a living congregation there is a deep relation between the preacher and the community. The line of impact for Christ is from the man in the pulpit to the man in the pew to the man in the street.

When we offer the gifts of our hands, the bread and wine taken from nature and human industry, and our very bodies, these things are not changed; but we realize that they are creative instruments in our hands for God's use and for the good of all men. In such giving we know ourselves as priests with Christ—not merely in the sense that we have access to God without the mediation of saints and other men, but also in the sense that we are Christs to one another and to the world.

A catholic congregation is one that broods over the whole life of the community it serves and offers the whole community and the whole world to God. Where committed concern is real, evangelism can be left to look after itself—ways to communicate will present themselves, and these will be the most effective channels. It is a false differentiation to speak of the church's congregational expression on the one hand and of its evangelistic mission on the other.

THE BRIDGE-BUILDING COMMUNITY

A congregation is not a club of respectable people but the home of the school of saints and sinners. It can hope to be catholic to the degree that human differences within the fellowship are overcome in Christ. Differences of age, race, education, and social status are not merely ". . . annulled as if they did not exist or did not matter. They are overcome through our free self-offering in the spirit of Christ—a free self-offering that otherwise we could not and would not make. As distinctions in fact, these differences continue; but now not as destructive forces in society but as occasions for fruitful tensions. . . . In His presence we find it possible to use our differences for mutual enrichment for the common task of living and to do away with those results of our differences which take the form of prejudice and suspicion and hostility." [11] The congregation that lives by that conviction and spirit can boldly proclaim, "Whoever will may come" because bridges of understanding and fellowship have been built and are continuing to be built in its own life.

Take the race question, for example. Whether you and the congregation to which you belong can honestly say that whoever will may come depends partly on your answers to the following questions: "Do I want the man across the street in my church whether he is white, Negro, Indian American, or Oriental; born on the mainland or in Puerto Rico? Am I willing to have persons of any of these groups in my pew, next to me at the communion rail, in the choir, as members of the church board? Would I be happy to have a person from another racial group as my pastor?"

Or consider other bridges of reconciliation. Dr. Conrad Bergendoff asks in *I Believe in the Church:*

Is it absurd to believe that you can bring in the Kingdom to the state legislature when you cannot make it apparent in the ladies' aid society, or the church choir? Or to put the case more pointedly, is the annual business meeting of a congregation typical of a Christian congress as some would make it? . . . Mind you, I do not say that the Church should be silent and inactive in these larger and wider spheres. What I am saying is that the Church is incompetent to do so until the local congregations are more perfect copies of what we would want the larger sphere to be. . . . If there is to be a regeneration of American communities, be it in metropolitan or in highway crossroads village, it must come from the small unit of a Christian congregation whose members have Christ as King in their lives.[12]

In other words, congregations must first of all bear witness to themselves—"To thine own self be true."

There are also the bridges of understanding and co-operation that must be built between the congregations in the community. There is sinful rivalry between many of them, and sometimes between congregations of the same denomination. Congregations that are busy controverting each other can hardly build bridges of understanding within the community. One labor-management group said to pastors who offered to arbitrate a strike and whose congregations were not on friendly terms, "Go and mend your own nets."

It is the role of the congregation to be the channel through which the work of God is done in the world, and particularly in its community. Every congregation has a number of activities. What matters most is that all of them, individually and together, proclaim the gospel. This can happen only when every gift, talent, and activity are first offered in genuine worship. Too often decisions by parish councils are inconsistent with the gospel proclaimed at worship. Too often the various organizations in the church operate at cross purposes or are unrelated to one another. All too often people leave the church because their feelings were hurt or because they didn't get their own way. This happens when groups within the congregation and individual members do not conceive of the congregation as the Body of Christ and participate only for self-serving ends.

In the rendition of a symphony what is it that matters most—losing one's self in the totality of the mighty sym-

phony or displaying one's own clever performance of a
difficult passage? It is reported that a soloist complained to
Arturo Toscanini because she was not given enough attention. When she said, "Are you forgetting that I am the star
of this performance?" Mr. Toscanini replied with character-
istic abruptness, "You are dismissed. There are no stars in
this performance." On another occasion, at a rehearsal, the
maestro put down his baton and said, "The piccolo isn't
quite coming through." In the mighty symphony of God
every player's part is important.

THE WITNESSING COMMUNITY

A congregation is not simply a company of witnesses to
the community—it is itself a witnessing community. The
witness of the individual must find its locus in the witness
of the congregation and the whole church. Effective evangelism is actually living in a Christian community. The
Christian community makes an evangelistic impact upon
individuals within it and upon communities surrounding it.

I quote from a letter I received recently from a New
York City pastor:

What is needed today is a resurgence of life and power in our
congregations. We have grown relatively weaker on the parish
level, despite our statistical successes. We have lost, to a degree,
our real concern for people. If concern for people were our
motivation, our parish planning would have to be scrutinized
very closely. Our programing would follow new and untried
directions. Our budgets would probably go much higher than
they are now. Our benevolences would double. We would also
discover that giving more than we are now giving would bring
us greater joy and blessing.

Concern for people would compel us to become personally involved in the lives of people we now avoid. It would compel us to give up many trivialities which now give us a false sense of being terribly busy with the Lord's affairs—which may not be the Lord's affairs at all! It would drive us to active participation in community affairs, of which we may now be blissfully ignorant. It would force us to do battle with unseen powers which wreck and destroy, to take a stand on issues where human values are involved. Then, too, the Lord would release new resources and new power in our individual lives, in our parishes, and throughout the church.

Spiritually concerned and alive congregations will expect to be called upon again and again for their time, their lives, and their money to help meet many needs. A congregation of lesser quality will be "tired of these appeals" almost before the appeals are made.

Ernest W. Southcott speaks of the congregation as a revolutionary community in *The Parish Comes Alive:* "When the parish is a community in which God is discovered and rediscovered, in which Christ is shown forth, in which the Holy Spirit is experienced, it is revolutionary and dynamic. It is a community in which people see more and more of the love of God and do more and more about it." [13] The power of transformation that God has vested in his Holy Spirit emerges before the eyes of men, if it emerges at all in the world, in the community. It manifests itself in the community in and through the congregation. There is something damning about a congregation when men and women can live within its shadows, when youth and children can play in its environs, without knowing anything about it except that it is a church and that some people go there on Sundays. The congregation is the Body of Christ when it passes on God's gifts of grace to all irrespective of race, education, age, class, culture.

Every congregation committed to being the Body of Christ in its community must know itself and its community. This calls for congregation and community self studies to secure self images of both. This is imperative not only for congregations in urban situations; every congregation needs a framework in which to see its role, including the scattered country parishes.

The congregation should study itself honestly from bottom to top. Pastor and laity will not be afraid to face their failures and ignorance if they desire to see more clearly what God wants the congregation to be and to be doing.

Inevitably they will be led to ask: Is our congregation meeting the needs and changes of our community? Are our programs, activities, and time schedules outdated? Are customs and practices still in operation that are no longer meaningful? Is our church a place where men find deep friendship, personal responsibility, wholeness of worship, transcendence of class and race divisions? Does the total parish program proclaim the gospel relevantly? Would it actually make any difference to the community if our church went out of existence? Obituaries have been written and will be written for those churches whose members do not seriously ask such questions and who are unwilling to search their hearts for both a present and a future alive with the promises of God and his kingdom.

At least five groups of facts are of prime importance:

1. Who are the people who live within the parish neighborhood or community?

The study of population is what sociologists call demography. Such a study correlates people and geography; and parish boundaries, regardless of how arbitrary they are, must be determined. However, since the church community may not be the work community or the recreational community, churches undertaking a study must work in co-operation with other congregations who share the same communities.

The demographic study includes population, economic status, educational status, age pyramid, and housing. The city or county authorities, the telephone company, market research people, the Chamber of Commerce, and other service agencies can be most helpful in drawing up a demographic picture of the parish. The purpose of the demographic study is to produce an "us" orientation between congregation and community rather than a "we-they" one.

2. What is the religious practice of the community?

Here, again, co-operation with other churches will be needed. The advantages of co-operation in this study should be obvious to all churches. All the congregations in the community should gather together and provide such minimal information as: What is the membership of the congregations living within the determined parish boundary? What percentage attend worship at least twice a month? What percentage never attend worship? What is the membership increase over the past three years? What is the average yearly attendance at worship? What is the Sunday school enrollment? What percentage attend with responsible regularity?

A spot check of church attendance on a given Sunday would be informative. The congregations may want to set aside more than one Sunday for spot checking. Unannounced one Sunday, every person present in every church in the area might be given a questionnaire as he enters the church with instructions that it should be filled out but not signed. Questions such as these are suggested: Do you belong to a church? If so, where? How often do you attend?

3. What is the depth of Christian thinking in the community?

This study calls for picking at random a number of persons to be interviewed. If such individuals from outside the community could be secured to conduct this part of the study, the chances are that the answers would be more honest and objective and the reporting less slanted. The questions asked should differ, depending on the person interviewed and—as the interview progresses—on answers he has given to previous questions. Suggested questions: Do you attend church? Why do you—or why don't you—attend? Are you personally acquainted with any of the pastors in this community? Do you feel that the churches help to build bridges of understanding between various groups in the community? Do the churches care about what happens to the community? As a parent, would you be willing for your child to make friends with another child who is known to have a police record? Would it make any difference to you if all the churches in this community closed their doors?

The purpose of this study is to determine to what extent the Christian viewpoint is present in the community.

4. What is the self-image of the congregation?

The congregation, and preferably all the congregations in the community, should plot on a map of the area the residences of members, Sunday school pupils, new members received over a five-year period, and leaders of the congregation. A population pyramid of church membership should be constructed, showing percentage in each age and sex group, and this should be related to the population pyramid of the community. There should be a graph of congregational mobility.

5. How do the members evaluate the congregation's attitude toward its neighborhood and people?

A selected number of lay leaders, parish councilmen, Sunday school teachers, and organizational leaders, and a corresponding number of church members who are not in leadership positions, should be given questions to be checked and returned to the leader of this part of the study.

A five-point study program of the type that has been suggested is not exhaustive, and only a thumbnail sketch has been presented to indicate direction. Getting the facts is important but not an end in itself. Congregations can be ". . . like a man who observes his natural face in a mirror . . . and goes away and at once forgets what he was like." [14]

Some months ago I became engaged in conversation with a man on a plane. He was a liaison representative of both labor and industry. I asked him what principles he used to guide him in his work. He replied, "There are four basic guideposts or principles and every one is as important as the other. And they are basic principles that can be helpful to denominations and to congregations in their planning. They are: First, get the facts, all the facts. No prejudging and no guesswork are permissible. Second, analyze and interpret the facts. Responsible people should be involved in this analysis. Facts and their interpretation provide the diagnoses.

Be as coldly objective as a research scientist. Third, make a decision. Decision making is not easy. In the case of the congregation it calls for group dynamics, informal conversation, and parish planning. And, fourth, make sure the decisions are put into operation. Here is the bottleneck for many congregations. Without decision making and decisions put into operation, the first two steps are harmful and should never be undertaken."

A periodic self inventory and religious census with a follow-up strategy in regard to lapsed, moved, and absent members, an outgoing evangelistic mission to reclaim and renew, an annual review of the church program and its effectiveness, a continuing study and planning committee with short term and long range goals and objectives, visitation of other congregations, conferences, and institutes—all these are means of keeping abreast of the times and making the mechanism of change operative in the organizational structure of the church. Creativity and innovation must be stimulated and encouraged, since the congregation that is concerned about its mission is the one willing to experiment and initiate—for Christ. It is not enough that people be gathered into churches, although this is basic, an assignment the church must ever seek to carry out more effectively. The kingdom of heaven is also like a leaven. Witnessing for Christ has a penetrating aspect. The witness for Christ must cause his Christ-like concern for the whole man to penetrate every human activity. As Dr. Martin E. Marty so incisively stated at a seminar, "A congregation is the front line of the church, the cutting edge of which must be sharp."

It was Frank Weston who said that we must ". . . relate the two communities, the congregation and the parish, otherwise we make nonsense of the Gospel. I believe we can do this best by getting alongside each other in our own street. We are right in the midst of social responsibility. We may be next door to an agnostic, or a Communist, and so we are right in the midst of the warfare of ideologies. If we are alive to our responsibilities for the person next door then we are more likely to see beyond the next door to our responsibilities in Kenya, Johannesburg, and Cyprus." [15]

The "church" is people and not buildings. We must restore the proper balance between the house of God and the people of God. It should be clear that wherever the people go, there the church goes. The members of a congregation are a gathered people when they come together for worship; they are a scattered people in the world. The local congregation, whether it be in the heart of the city, in the suburb, in the crossroad village, is the all important cell in the total organism of the church, and the worship and witness of the people are decisive.

Some time ago Rev. John Heuss of the Trinity Parish, New York, preached a sermon on "The True Function of a Parish." One paragraph expresses what we have tried to say:

The early church was like a beehive in reverse. There was much coming in and going out but the coming in was to get renewed strength from fellowship, prayer, and breaking of bread in order to take the precious way of salvation out to the uttermost parts of the earth.

The Word and the Sacraments are the bedrock on which we must build if we are to live the faith with a sense of exhilaration, feeling the transformation and renewal known to the early church and recaptured by the Reformation.

8:

CREATIVE APPROACHES
TO COMMUNITY

*I*n an increasing measure congregations are honestly appraising themselves and their communities and are discovering their own creative expressions, allowing the Spirit to blow "where it wills." [1] They keep asking themselves, "What is a congregation?" and "What is a congregation for?" These questions have inspired the more disturbing question, "What is the will of Christ for our congregation?"

Exciting experiments are being made. These vary considerably, since "God moves in a mysterious way, his wonders to perform." [2] Yet there is marked similarity because the mission of every congregation is the same. One pastor commented, "The church that seeks to serve its Lord is continually searching for new patterns that will communicate the gospel. Such searching is the necessity of every congregation. But it comes as a gift from God."

In describing some approaches of congregations to their communities I have purposely omitted identifying them either by naming the communities where they are located or by indicating their denominational affiliations. The case studies are samplings only. They are not "success stories."

There are no successful congregations. These are congregations that are living in and serving their communities, seeking to turn eyes and hearts to God. As one layman expressed it, "We have not learned all the answers, but we have learned that God is faithful and that his word works miracles." His pastor added, "We do rejoice that we have been unhampered in our approaches and have not been required to conform to programs conceived by others. At the same time we acknowledge how much we have learned from others, and we do share fellowship with the whole church."

With Dietrich Bonhoeffer, they have learned that only they who give thanks for little things receive the big things:

If we do not give thanks daily for the Christian fellowship in which we have been placed, even where there is no great experience, no discoverable riches, but much weakness, small faith, and difficulty; if on the contrary, we only keep complaining to God that everything is so paltry and petty, so far from what we expected, then we hinder God from letting our fellowship grow according to the measure and riches which are there for us all in Jesus Christ.[3]

OPERATION ONE MILE

A congregation in the East has in the last ten years "ripped off its horse blinkers to get its eyes on the precious souls living at its doors in the inner city." The new phase began with Operation One Mile—a strategy for the congregation's self determined boundary of intensive witness and service.

The story of the project is fascinating:

We flooded the mailboxes of the twenty thousand people who lived in this pocket with pictorial folders and invitations. We set up a telephone evangelism effort aimed at penetrating apartments and residences that are out of bounds to church visitors. We set out to learn what institutions were here and found nursing homes where inmates were vegetating. We learned of Alcoholics Anonymous centers and presented ourselves. We studied population mobility, family income ranges, the percentage of colored and white residents, long range plans for renewal and how they would affect us, new inner city expressways, the juvenile delinquency pattern, and the unmarried mother ratio. We recognized that we were privileged and singled out to witness here to Christ as Lord and Savior.

So we plunged in with eyes wide open to the toughness of our problem. Children of the community are now in our Sunday school. Our children's choir is variegated in color. There are healthy turnouts to parish teachers' nights. Two services are held every Sunday morning. We walk on air these days as we carry on an expanding program in our new educational building and parish house. There is a growing corps of lay apostles. The shut-ins of the congregation and community are visited by both adults and youth. 'Gangs' have been formed to help aged with their chores, and those with fading eyesight are read to and helped to the clinic. There is a full-orbed teaching program for children, youth, and adults. Healing services are held. A recent adult instruction-for-membership class included five Negroes, an orthodox Jew, a convert from Buddhism, an Indonesian, and a redeemed alcoholic. In years we are an old congregation, but, by the indwelling of the Holy Spirit, we are new in spirit and hopeful about tomorrow.

This congregation is self-sustaining and has given assistance—with members and money—to three new congregations in its suburban area. It also gives financial support, over and above its benevolence allocation through its denominational board of world missions, to two missionaries. Two pastors, a parish worker, a secretary, a minister of music, and a sexton constitute the staff.

FILLED WITH NEW SURENESS

An "old" congregation located in an area of high mobility and transition has since 1956 been served by a pastor who came from Puerto Rico. In that year the membership of the congregation was 103 souls, principally of German and Nordic descent, most of whom lived far from the church. There was no Sunday school.

The congregation now serves its community. The membership is two hundred, but twenty-eight of these are Puerto Rican, fifteen are Negro, five are Chinese, and eight are Jewish in background. The Sunday school now numbers sixty community children from a great variety of racial and cultural backgrounds. In 1958 the congregation more than doubled its benevolences—from $1,400 in 1957 to $3,800 in 1958. The pastor says: "It shows that one of the best ways to help oneself is to help others." The pastor plays an active role in the community and he often meets with individuals and groups who are concerned with community problems. He is active in the urban renewal program.

As for the over-all response, the pastor makes this observation, "Some rumblings of discontent are heard. A few members would rather close the doors than radically reorient themselves to a community ministry. But many have been reborn as Christians as they have agonized over the problems of integration and participated in this new interracial community. Again and again, as we were in the midst of despair over human pettiness and prejudice, the Holy Spirit has broken through, filling us with a new sureness that the faithful church has available to it the very power of God."

FACING UP TO ITS FUTURE

A congregation established in 1873 reached its peak before World War I and then declined steadily as the members moved away. Now it stands between a Polish Roman Catholic settlement and a section increasingly populated by Negroes from the South.

In 1953 the congregation faced four choices: (1) sell to a Negro congregation and move away; (2) merge with another church of its denomination; (3) disband; or (4) develop a ministry in Christ's name to the inhabitants of the neighborhood. After much thought and prayer it was decided that the church had a mission to its neighborhood.

The congregation now represents a cross section of the neighborhood. Negro members have been elected to the boards of deacons, Christian education, and the Women's Guild. A Negro member is secretary of the congregation. With the help of college-age workers in the summer, camping programs on a nearby camp site have been developed.

The budget for the two hundred members is $13,500 annually, with $2,500 for benevolences.

The pastor of the congregation affirms these principles for a church that wants to serve an inner city area:

1. It must be prepared to be a mission, to think mission, and to see the reason for the church as mission, with its primary purpose outreach.

2. Its first responsibility must be for its immediate parish area and the people who live in it.

3. It must have a clergy willing to live in the area.

THE SUBURB, TOO

A pastor in a suburban community writes:

Our parish approach to revival is centered in Word and Sacrament. Attendance in 1954 was forty-five; now (1959) we average 125. Two services are held, with the celebration of the Sacrament at the early service. People stop in to pray during the week, since the church is never locked. Matins are held daily.

We have no money-making schemes. The support is greater now in six weeks than it used to be for the whole year. All children attend worship except the nursery and kindergarten children, and they attend once each month.

We stress that this is a community church for all people. The PTA-sponsored Girl Scout troop meets in our educational center. The PTA has luncheons and other affairs in the center. A Girl Scout Council meets monthly there. A teen-age youth canteen is held there each week, and only six of the fifty who attend are our "kids." Young adults use our center for monthly social meetings. The hot rod club meets weekly in the center, and only two of the twenty-five are members of the parish. The center is also available for private parties (graduation, birthday, and so forth) to any group in the community willing to pay for heat and light.

ECUMENICAL DIALOGUE

In a New York town, population two thousand, six congregations, including the Roman Catholic Church, engaged in a five session ecumenical dialogue. A lay participant reported:

All who shared in the group wanted to learn the doctrine of each denomination and the reasons for the different practices in each church. We wanted to know why people decided to become members of a particular church aside from its being a family tradition. There was not sufficient time for this in our study group but it was uppermost in the minds of those attending. We felt that a better understanding of practices and principles in each church made for greater unity in Christ. This, no doubt, will be a starting point if the study group convenes again.

It would appear that such dialogues have real possibilities. In most communities the chances are that the Roman Catholic Church would not be a participant. If ecumenical dialogue does not begin to take place on the local level, world and national councils of churches will not be particularly effective. Furthermore, dialogue affords an excellent opportunity to discover what the denominational articulation of the faith really is. More important, the catholic faith might be discovered in the process.

THE URBAN COMMISSION APPROACH

A few years ago, a cathedral church appointed an Urban Commission composed of ten people, with two requirements for membership; they must be active in the congregation and they must be convinced about integration.

Each member of the commission heads up one of its ten subcommittees and has power to co-opt others to work with him. The responsibilities of five of these subcommittees are particularly noteworthy.

Program Planning: The neighborhood is in process of major changes, which include a new expressway and the construction of a major medical center in the immediate community. The group charged with program planning must look ahead and suggest what future adaptation in the church's program may be indicated by these changes. They also make recommendations to other sections of the commission on immediate action and on experimentation with new approaches and new groups.

Neighborhood Bible Classes and Services: There are about a dozen such classes, most of them under lay leadership. The pastor reports that last year, after four years of such classes, the first converts were received from the groups and "Now almost all neighborhood people who come to Bible classes come to church, and many have been united with the congregation. Only occasionally do we celebrate Holy Communion at these house meetings—then it is done with the liturgical movement emphasis."

Preaching Missions: A major preaching mission aimed at the community is conducted every two years.

Instruction Classes: The pastor states, "We own a large house next to the cathedral, where we do what we can for all our organizations. In walking weather we have volunteers who sit at the entrance serving coffee and giving information to inquirers. There is an Inquirers' Class that meets Sunday nights from 6 to 8 P.M., led by the clergy. Considerable literature is distributed."

Neighborhood Callers: About twenty people have taken a course lasting sixteen weeks on how to call on people; how to bring them to church; and so on. One of the clergy writes:

We reach one in twenty, and about one in forty are eventually brought into the fellowship of the church by these people. What we do, and our approach, boils down to our doctrine of the church. If it is to proclaim the word, to heal the sick, and to teach men about God, we make one approach; and if we believe something else about the nature of the church we do something else. If the inner city church is to become an indigenous church, it must go into the highways and hedges, the streets and alleys, with the message that God cares and is concerned—period!

LITURGICAL ACTION

A chapel in the worst slum area of a large city, with support of the mother congregation, has been used to create an urban missionary program based on liturgical action. The postulations of the work are:

1. Human relations are primarily resolved in baptism, confirmations, and Holy Communion, making all of one blood in the spirit.

2. The spiritual and social life of the people must be closely interwoven with neighborhood agencies.

3. The church must witness to unity in God and refuse to become an exclusively Negro, Chinese, or Italian congregation, or exclusively a middle income or rich one.

4. The chapel must witness with such outward signs as: church doors open; bells rung for daily services; processions on the street; ceremonial planting of church crosses on Rogation Sunday (Rural Life Sunday); the blessing of the tenements by the priest at Christmas and Easter time.

5. For the future health of the parish and the church at large, concentration of the ministry to the immediate community is imperative. Distant communicants cannot be depended upon for sustained participation, and sentimental parochialism is a handicap.

One observer said, "In five years these principles have proved to be a sound basis for an ever expanding ministry to this community."

A DOWNTOWN PARISH

A downtown church, organized in 1874, made a study of its membership. The study showed that every activity was "down." There seemed to be but one solution—to relocate. But there were other factors that nagged at the leaders of this old church. "Hundreds of children in our community are unchurched. . . . Many persons living, working, and passing through downtown need spiritual counseling. . . . Staff and other workers at the growing Medical Center near here need to be served."

Three years ago the congregation decided to remain downtown. Instead of retreating, the church has completed a $150,000 addition and has revamped its entire program.

THE NEW BIRTH OF A CONGREGATION

It is a thrill to be involved in the new birth of a congregation which has sought and found the answers to such questions as: To whom does the church belong? For whom is the gospel meant?

All the problems have not been solved. All the difficulties have not been overcome. We do not yet see all that God has in store for this congregation. What we do see is the emergence of a congregation dedicated as never before to God's program and purpose for his church—a fellowship of believers who are concerned with bearing witness to the gospel of Jesus Christ that all men might be saved.

It is when pastors and members of congregations get the pattern of the church confused with its mission that progress stops. The mission often demands that the pattern be changed. We have learned and are continuing to learn the difference between pattern and mission.

This is the testimony of a pastor whose church is in a community whose population has changed from all white to 60 per cent Negro in four and a half years. The effect of the change is seen in the congregation's statistics. In the two years, 1957-1958, this congregation lost 112 confirmed members or more than one third of its membership. Morale of the members was low as they saw Sunday school and worship attendance decline, leadership potential lessen, and income decrease. The pastor's testimony indicates that the congregation came to grips with its mission and by the grace of God the congregation was reborn. He added, "I think we've been hurt as much as we're going to be hurt. I am optimistic for the future of the parish."

This congregation effected the change without requesting subsidy and without importing staff assistance.

A BLOCK PARTY

A congregation in an Eastern city gives the following account of its block party experiment in community identification:

The parish sponsored an old-fashioned block party, with the police department roping off our streets. Over five hundred people participated, the greatest majority of them our Jewish neighbors. The response was overwhelming, and we have been asked to sponsor another such party very soon. Plans are already under way for the next one.

Young and old danced in the street and special entertainment was provided by neighborhood "kids." The pastor feels that the block party helped to break down many barriers and has also created a real community spirit on the block. The pastor cannot walk down the street without someone coming up to him and asking, "Rev., when is the next block party?" and "Is there anything I can do to help?" One Jewish dentist on the street was so impressed that he personally called on the pastor and offered to do free dental work for underprivileged children in the parish.

AGAIN MISSION

One congregation, through careful study of itself and its all-white community, discovered in 1954 that only 15 per cent of its members lived within a mile of its church building. It discovered also that the immediate six-block area was 40 per cent unchurched. The divorce of church and community through the years was painfully evident and the handwriting was on the wall. The congregation faced itself and its mission and went to work prayerfully, thoughtfully, carefully, and obediently. Today 45 per cent of the members live within a mile of the church, many new members are from the immediate neighborhood, and scores have been transferred to churches in their own neighborhoods.

The pastor commented, "This congregation is no longer just *interested* in missions. It has again *become* mission."

PLANTED IN THE INNER CITY

"Many city churches flee to suburbia when their neighborhoods become depressed," begins a report on a church in a large city, "This church was born in a lower income, racially mixed section of the city. More than two-thirds of its members live in a public-housing project. Most churches center their activities in a building. A high proportion of this congregation's program is spread around the community. While most congregations worship together only on Sunday, this congregation also worships during the week in members' homes."

A church reporter described this young congregation, organized in March, 1958, as follows:

That pastor states that "in our church we have worked together in house-churches ever since our beginning three years ago. Now we feel ready and required to go a step further and divide our fairly well defined parish into three zones, each of which will form a house-church for the members who live in their zone. Each house-church will be responsible for evangelism in its zone—through person-to-person work, through visitations, through invitations to come, and through just being in the neighborhood on a regular basis. Only in terms of a total community in the church will people see the church to be relevant to their life in the local community and world—a life of broken relationships."

And here is a bit of history. The work was started in a building basement that had been occupied by a dissolved Slovak church. Into that unpromising, not to say impossible, situation came the pastor and his family, and *into* it they came, moving right into the middle of a racially mixed neighborhood. Soon the pastor had coaxed forty-nine people, divided between whites and Negroes, into his house churches. And that was how a church was born where a church had been dying.

An observer comments that this church discovered a way to integrate colors, races, and economic groups into a rare brotherhood in Christ. One member, when asked about integration, replied, "I don't believe that people think of it as 'integrated,' but simply as 'church.' You hardly ever think about there being any distinctions in the congregation."

The congregation knows the meaning of oneness in its total life. That oneness finds expression in house-church, community, love for one another.

"CLAWS OUT" ITS MEMBERSHIP

This is the story of one of the oldest Protestant churches in the East. In 1957 a new church building was erected at a cost of $232,000. The full time staff that directs the program of the congregation includes the pastor, a vicar, a secretary, and a day school teaching staff. Dedicated laymen are active in the entire program.

The pastor reports that the mobility rate in the neighborhood is so high that the essential membership of the church is new every five years. "Yet the congregation remains strong. In order to keep numerical strength, it becomes necessary to 'claw out' a membership from an area of rock-imbedded indifference." The pastor's strong leadership through twenty-five years is coupled with the conviction that a church must serve its community, that the gospel with which it is charged is a gospel for all men, and that this goes beyond lip service.

The church is located in an area of apartment dwellings. It has divided its community into four sections; four times a year each section is approached with literature and invitations. Many children, young people, and adults are involved in this program. Approximately 16,000 calls are made annually. The response has been slow but effective in a nominally Roman Catholic and Jewish community. There are almost one hundred former Jews in the parish family. Thirty-three different ethnic backgrounds and races are represented in the membership.

People of Jewish background serve on the church board. A former Jew is the congregation's secretary. Church school teachers include several Negroes and Puerto Ricans. A

Puerto Rican is the church school superintendent. People of Italian and Greek background also teach in the church school, as did a Chinese and a Japanese before they moved out of the community. The choir includes twelve Negroes and several persons of Jewish background.

The pastor feels that he and the congregation must be a real part of the community:

> The pastor will not be effective in the community until he has learned the temper of the community, come to know why the people act as they do. The church must make itself known in the community and assume community responsibility. The constantly changing neighborhood need not affect the church adversely if it is alert to its calling and nature as a church. Such a church must face up to its problems. The congregation should not, however, be left to stand alone, but the national church bodies must begin to support the inner city church. Only in this way will churches be able to remain in their communities and continue ministries in those communities.

A POSITIVE APPROACH TO THE RURAL COMMUNITY

Many congregations in rural communities are in a bad way because of negative attitudes. By contrast, the pastor of one effective rural congregation expresses this wholesome approach toward the responsibility of the church in a village where he is serving:

> The real crop of our country is people, the people who grew up here and live here, the people who move here and stay here, the people who grew up here and leave to make their contribution to other, mostly urban, communities. The real role of our country is not to produce the best possible wheat, cattle, and milk—but more important, to produce the best people. Urban

areas all over our nation need the vigorous, healthy, normal boys and girls that we produce. The future leaders of our nation are growing up right now in communities like ours. The destiny of the nation depends on our country and hundreds of other communities like it. The quality of our main crop, people, is about all that is going to count for much in the long run.

A CONGREGATION IN LITTLE ITALY

A congregation was organized fifty years ago in a near downtown area known as Little Italy. About 90 per cent of the congregation is Italian. There are 325 adult members, most of them of Roman Catholic background. They have an excellent complex of buildings, with church, parish hall, and educational center. Considerable emphasis is given to community service. The congregation sponsors a day school, health center, adult education, and athletic program.

The main emphasis of the program are:

1. To gain the confidence of the community—though the area is largely Roman, the people have confidence that the church is there to serve them.

2. To witness as individual members—many of the members are called upon to defend their faith and have enabled others to find Christ and be united in the fellowship of the church.

3. To make a community effort—through a well rounded community program many doors are opened to serve people in their daily lives.

PARISH WHOLENESS

On the border between the luxury buildings on the avenue and the poorer section across the way stands Trinity Church. Six years ago, after a prolonged vacancy in the pastorate, a

minister was assigned to the church. Its dwindling membership was widely dispersed with only three church families
living in the neighborhood. Surveys showed that 76 per cent
of the residents were of Jewish faith. The back streets were
populated by Negroes, Puerto Ricans, and others of Latin
American, Irish, and Italian background. Housing conditions
were approaching blight proportions. To the casual observer, it seemed the church was "dying."

The pastor's diagnosis of the situation: "The church was
not dying. It was killing itself because of lack of concern for
the people on the doorsteps. Its spirit and outlook was that
of a social club; it had forgotten to be the church of Jesus
Christ."

The problems of this congregation were not unlike those
that confront most other parishes: how to activate in the
faithful a spirit of concern for the community with its vast
unchurched population; how to improve the congregation's
total stewardship; how to deepen the spiritual life of its
members; how to boost the service organizations; above all,
how to be the church!

The emphasis of the parish is on wholeness—the whole
Bible, the whole congregation, the whole person, the whole
community.

A comprehensive survey of the community was made, with
visitation in every home to which access could be gained.
The church was renovated, and an attempt was made to
have everything speak of the presence of God. The full service of Word and Sacrament was restored to its central place
in the parish life. Every Wednesday of the year a growing
number of adults now gather for study of the Bible. There is
today only one auxiliary organization of the congregation.

The pastor believes that this unity of organizational life is a corollary of the sacramental unity of the church of Christ. The programs are on churchly themes geared to the whole family and are followed by periods of entertainment.

"Without elaborate programing," comments the pastor, "and without direct 'money' preaching, the contributions of the people have tripled, the downward trend in membership has been halted, and today the majority of the present membership live in the vicinity of the church building. Trinity is now a community church, and its people represent the various races and national groups in the neighborhood."

"Wholeness" is the word the characterizes this congregation. The congregation simply came to see that the duty of the whole congregation is to make the whole gospel available to the whole community.

A PASTORAL LETTER

As the steward of the mysteries of God, the pastor is expected to preach the word in season and out of season and seek to make the word relevant if he is to care for the flock committed to him. He is called to faithfulness, not to success. Those who never sell the message short are the real heroes of the faith.

Recently a pastor laid bare his heart to his people in a letter, and therein revealed a true shepherd's spirit. The letter reads as follows:

What are Redeemer's chances in its present location? Is it really true that Redeemer's days are numbered? Does the densely populated, interracial, run-down, and blighted neighborhood present a soil in which our church cannot operate successfully? . . .

For years we have heard people say, "Redeemer's days are numbered" or "We must relocate to survive," or "It is futile and foolish to attempt expansion in an area as blighted as ours."

It is my conviction that our greatest assets—for we might well be envied—lie precisely in those factors that we frequently deprecate as liabilities. Redeemer is located in the very heart of the most densely populated area between Chicago and San Francisco. While other churches lack and search for population concentrations in which to labor as an effective leaven, we have such vast mission opportunities that they stagger the imagination. Who would be so foolish as to say, "Let us leave this bumper crop to seek out a field which is sparse and thin?" Since the living church must have people to redeem before it can carry out the Savior's redemptive work, Redeemer should thank God on its knees for the vast field with which our Lord has blessed us.

You say, "But our neighborhood is a vice-ridden, crime-breeding neighborhood, a festering ulcer on the body metropolis!" You are so correct! It is all of that and much more. But have you forgotten what we are? We are a church; we are Christ's Body: we are other Christs. Did not our blessed Lord come into the world precisely for the purpose of invading the dimensions of crime and corruption, death and decay, sin and sickness, for the purpose of cleansing the leper, healing the sick, restoring the lost? If there is any neighborhood about which the redeeming Christ is pre-eminently concerned, that neighborhood is ours. If there is a seething mass of sick humanity that the loving Christ wants to love back into the dignity and sanctity of the Father's bosom, that mass of humanity is at our doorstep.

And what shall we say about the fact that our neighborhood is populated largely by Negroes, Mexicans, Orientals, Indians, and others? Does not this give us excellent warrant for moving out?— Oh friend, what are you thinking of? There are many congregations that can preach and teach about racial tolerance but very rarely have an opportunity to practice it. Redeemer has the blessed privilege every Sunday and every day of living its protestation of faith. Here we can clasp the hand of our Negro and Oriental brother. Here at Redeemer the white, the black, the yellow, and the red can kneel together at the communion rail while the Common Chalice unites us all in the Body of that Christ who came to seek and to save humanity.

And now, what are Redeemer's chances? Or, shall we say, what are Christ's chances to do his work through Redeemer?

After touring Manhattan with members of denominational boards of missions, Rev. Heinrich Herman Ulrick, a German official, said:

I was struck by the contrast—the multi-million dollar buildings of downtown Manhattan and the appalling decay and dirt of Harlem's tenements; wealth and want living door to door. And then I saw those old churches stemming the tide of new population pressures, their readiness to serve without asking about returns from investments of money and effort and sacrifice. I met young pastors ready to move into homes Europeans would consider unfit to live in. I'll carry with me the image of the church of America when I return home—a church on the frontier of social change.

A congregation, if it is to be the Body of Christ in the community and true to its all embracing mission, must consist of all sorts and conditions of men. It is not a religious ghetto. It reaches out to all people in love and it is the community's most open society. The congregation's mission as it confronts a community is nothing less than the salvation of everyone. When that is a congregation's passion the Holy Spirit breaks through creatively and sustainingly.

9:

THE PRIESTHOOD
OF THE LAYMAN

An experienced sea captain was invited by the president of a steamship company to inspect a new ship. It was a luxury ship, equipped and appointed magnificently. After the inspection the president asked, "Well, Captain, how do you like it?" The captain replied, "It is by all odds the finest ship I have even seen." Putting his hand on the captain's shoulder, and with a smile of satisfaction, the president said, "It is your ship. You are the captain." The captain pulled himself to attention and said, "Ships are all right, sir, but it is the men who are in them that count."

Churches, parish houses, educational buildings, programs, and plans are all right, but it is the people of God who really count. It is to living men and women that the Lord of the church has entrusted the gospel for delivery to all men. All the people of God are in God's service—all are on the same staff.

God calls, equips, and sends out living men and women to extend his kingdom. All are called to special service, none to special privilege.

The reawakening of the church to its vocation as mission

has brought with it a need to clarify the role of the minister and the role of the layman. And out of the process of clarification has come a fresh study of one of the cardinal principles of the Reformation: the concept of the church as the priesthood of believers.

The priesthood of all Christian believers is explicitly set forth in ". . . like living stones be yourselves built into a spiritual house, to be a holy priesthood, to offer spiritual sacrifices acceptable to God through Jesus Christ" [1] and ". . . you are a chosen race, a royal priesthood, a holy nation, God's own people, that you may declare the wonderful deeds of him who called you out of darkness into his marvelous light." [2]

As the people of God, Christians constitute a priesthood in which every member shares in Christ's mission. In the New Testament, to be a member of the laity is to be a member of a royal priesthood. This is such a high standing in its own God-given right that no office held within the universal priesthood can rank above it. To be a Christian is therefore infinitely more important than to be a clergyman. The church is a priestly society in respect to its whole membership. It is not a clerical society. Distinctions within the Christian fellowship are quite insignificant compared to the all-important distinction of being "in Christ" or "out of Christ."

Whether Christ established any specific structure for the church or any gradations in office will remain the subject of endless dispute. But there can be no question about the call to full service that he issued to all the people or about the kingly resources that he placed at their disposal for this service.

Whatever he said with rich overtones about himself in his vocation he said with the same rich overtones about his people and their vocation. He did say, "I am the light of the world." [3] He said also, "You are the light of the world." [4] He said that he performed "mighty works," but he also said, ". . . greater works than these will he the believing disciple do, because I go to the Father." [5] He spoke of his own mission into the world as the sent one of the Father, but he said also, "As the Father has sent me, even so I send you." [6] And when his own mission was finished on earth, he entrusted the entire work of the kingdom on earth to his people, "Go . . . and make disciples of all nations." [7] It was a mission of such magnitude that it could not be accomplished without the participation of the entire membership. At the same time he said, ". . . apart from me you can do nothing." [8] The greatest asset of the mission is expressed in the words, ". . . lo, I am with you always." [9]

One of the six subtopics for the Second Assembly of the World Council of Churches in 1954 was The Laity: The Christian in His Vocation. In the introduction to the report of the survey made on this subject is the statement:

It is through its lay membership that the Church enters into real and daily contact with the workaday world and shares in its problems and aspirations. It is in the life and work of the lay membership that the Church must manifest in the world its regenerative and redemptive power. One of the greatest tasks of the Church today is to grasp clearly the significance of the lay ministry in the world. [10]

The name "priests" belongs to all believers with equal authority and right. Through Christ all those who believe in him are "kings and priests unto God." Christ conveys to each of them all the treasures he has given to the church: "For all things are yours, whether Paul or Apollos or Cephas or the world or life or death or the present or the future, all are yours; and you are Christ's; and Christ is God's." [11]

To be sure, God has given his gifts that ". . . some should be apostles, some prophets, some evangelists, some pastors and teachers," but they were given "for the equipment of the saints" in order that they, the saints—the laity—might carry out "the work of the ministry." [12] The role of the pastor is to preach the word of God with faithfulness; to administer the sacraments; and to instruct, train, equip, and release the laity to be full-time ministers of Jesus Christ in the world, where the church has its God-given mission.

Hence, the ministry of the pastor is representative, since all Christians as priests share in that ministry. It is not the clergy who go into all the world. It is the layman who moves in upon the world, making contact at every point. The forward movement of the cause of Christ, the work of evangelism, the Christianization of society—this is the vocation of the Christian laymen whose daily work brings them into contact with all groups and all sorts and conditions of men. The pastor ". . . exists in the church for the sake of the world, and the laity exists in the world for the sake of the church." [13]

If the church is really to be the church—exist for the sake of the world and assume its servant nature—the ministry of the church must be the ministry of the laity bearing witness to the Lordship of Jesus Christ in all areas of life.

Unfortunately we seem to have narrowed the meaning of church work to congregational activity. While we should never minimize the service within and to the fellowship, we must nevertheless think of this service in its larger dimensions. The essential work of the Christian is to serve Christ in his home, in the work by which he makes his living, in his community, and in all his associations, thus redeeming those areas of the world's life. That is the true work of the church and the ministry of all believers. Meaningful church work is simply living for Christ every day, wherever we are.

The ministry of the laity must not only be recognized but also prepared for. The pastor then becomes a chief counselor to the congregation of priests.

When laymen and laywomen assemble during the week it should not be for the purpose of being preached at yet again or of being entertained, but for the purpose of undergoing serious training as witnesses of Christ and of realistically devising strategies for consolidating victories or for establishing new beachheads on behalf of the Church in our communities and in our culture.[14]

Individual reading, prayer, meditation, and solid thinking are essential. Laymen's series of books that have been and are being published by the churches are helpful. At the same time individual study needs to be checked and broadened by study and dialogue with other Christians. Laymen need to meet with other laymen in study groups. Pastors need give and take discussions with laymen for their own sake as well as for the sake of the laymen, if they are to know the world in which laymen live, the world into which they bring their priesthood. In such discussions and dialogue pastors will learn to communicate in language that the world will understand.

A leading Presbyterian layman complained about the irrelevance of theological discussions carried on at the Evans-

ton Assembly of the World Council of Churches, where
the voice of the laity was hardly heard. Yet laymen, he stated,
are the bridge over which the gospel must pass from the
sanctuary to society. The need for pastor-layman understanding was indicated by another layman—a grocer—who
said to his pastor, "I wonder if you know how hard it is for
me to make an altar out of my grocery counter." Do pastors
really know how hard it is for laymen to make altars out of
laboratories, law benches, city halls, lecture platforms, laun-
dry tubs, investment tables? Somehow pastors must know,
in order to help their people understand that Christian living
is the offering of life to the Father of life, to whom it belongs; a willingness to take their place in the vast operations
of his Spirit, instead of trying to run little businesses on
their own.

There are already, in every congregation, groups holding
regular meetings in which this serious training should be
taking place: meetings of church school teachers, the parish
council, the parish cabinet (leaders of auxiliaries), evangelism and stewardship committees, Bible classes, young adults,
senior citizens, Scout leaders and their committees. In a recent parish life dialogue a layman said, "The reason our
congregation is so dynamic is that we are all involved in the
life and mission of the parish. We support the pastor and the
pastor supports us. We are in the work together." Many
congregations have experimented gratifyingly with the
house church, parish retreats, school of life courses, the
academy approach and cell groups in which unchurched
people have been participants. One pastor channels people
who come to him for counsel into a cell group where problems germane to particular concerns are under discussion.

The exercising of one's priesthood in the various orders of society is neither easy nor spectacular. In fact, there are areas that the organized church may not be able to penetrate. For example, the church as a church may not be able to reach organized labor, or the professional society, or the social agencies, or the public schools, or the various social and professional fraternities and clubs. However, individual Christians, as members of these organized groups, can get through to them. If the early Christians could, by being "saints in Caesar's household" win others to Christ, then it can be done today. Indeed, it is being done over and over again by committed Christians. With St. Paul we can be all things to all men if we share his motive ". . . that I might by all means save some." [15]

A COMMITTED LAITY

To appreciate the priesthood of believers as the people of God is to see that every person, regardless of his work or station, is a priest of God to the extent that he takes the faith and the fellowship seriously. Charles Duell Kean observes in *The Christian Gospel and the Parish Church:*

In one sense he is a priest of some God whatever he does, and he shows it by what he does and how he does it. The father or mother dealing with their marriage or guiding their children, the business man in his office, the workman at his bench, the teacher in the class room, the citizen at the polling place or the community forum—all these in their several functions are exercising a priesthood.

Since it is in these practical areas that the Christian faith comes to life through enabling people to appreciate the range and depth of judgment and the forgiveness available through faith in

Jesus Christ, it is in these areas that the Christian Church shows itself to be a saved and saving fellowship. If the ministry of the pulpit and the altar, the pastor's study and the parish house is not functionally related to this wider and more incisive priesthood, then it is either a kind of medicine-man business, or there is nothing to distinguish it from directing a secular social agency.[16]

The language of priesthood used in the New Testament applies to all the members of the body. The priesthood enters into every phase of life. All are offered—work, home life, leisure, investments, spending, politics, friendships—since a priest must have something to offer through Christ to God. That is the priesthood of believers. Priesthood is the prerogative of all Christians. It derives from the church and inheres in the membership of the body.

It is of the essence then that laymen and laywomen recognize that they are more than bankers, mechanics, housewives, nurses, engineers, farmers, professors, day laborers, labor union leaders, industrialists. Life is more than food and the body more than clothing; and a man ought to be more than his profession or job. No Christian can hold back his witness with the excuse, "I am only a layman." He is a baptized layman. He belongs to God. He is committed. He is a priest of God.

One layman said, "We have been sealed with his name upon us, and nothing is alien to him or his understanding. If we are to walk with courage in an alien world, we, as Christian lay-people, are to walk in the knowledge that we do represent him, God help us! We are the church, wherever we are, and whoever we are, because we have received something that makes a difference. We did not invent it— we caught it, like an infection, from the body to which we belong—and it is a healthy infection. It is the infection that overcomes the infection that would destroy us."

Every individual responds in person to the call of God and bears fruit in his life to the glory of Christ who called him out of darkness into glorious light. No one crashes the gates and no one earns his way into the fellowship. The Lord Christ makes this unquestionably clear: "You did not choose me, but I chose you and appointed you." [17] Once we have resonded, our vocation is clear and unequivocal—to live responsibly before God and our fellow men.

"All the earth worships thee" [18] means what it says. Thus the old woman in the legend could boil her potatoes to the glory of God. Sister Theresa, serving in the kitchen, found him among the pots and pans she used. Bach could begin every composition with "To the glory of God" and end with "In the name of Jesus. Amen." The surgeon could say as he was about to perform an operation, "I pray that I might be used to save a life." Each of them made an altar out of his life and service. As priests they knew what it meant to ". . . present your bodies as a living sacrifice." [19]

Our place is not the auditorium but the stage—the field, the workshop, the laboratory, the school, the senate chamber, the kitchen, and wherever life touches life. God made us and redeemed us in order to use us in the most profitable way, for his purpose, not for ours.

10:

EDGE OF

THE EDGE

*I*n the RCA Building in New York City four murals depict the destiny of the human race. Three of them show the conquests of man and the fourth shows a lonely Cross on a bleak hill with humanity looking hopefully to it. Underneath, these words are inscribed, "Man's ultimate destiny depends not upon whether he can learn new lessons and make new discoveries and conquests, but on his acceptance of the lesson taught him two thousand years ago."

The cross was planted firmly in history, and in Christ's own life there were limitations that he accepted—being like man in all things. He accepted the givenness of the world situation into which the Father had sent him. The servant is not greater than his Lord: we no more live in an ideal world than he did. What we have to decide, as he did, is how to do the Father's will in our given situation in history, whatever the cost.

In seeking to do the Father's will we are humbled by the fact that he placed the torch of faith in our weak hands, to make it evident to everyone that salvation does not come from us but from him.

This world of ours will want more than pious memories of the Man on the Cross to set it right. It is the undeniable lesson of church history that where the church itself fails to live under the Cross it fails utterly and has no message to proclaim and no witness to give.

There are four things the church, living under the Cross, cannot do:

1. The church cannot win out against the world as if it were an organism apart trying to beat the world at its own power-and-prestige game. The church cannot compete against the world because God, who is Lord of the church, made the world. He holds it in his hands.

2. The church cannot despise the world or separate itself from the world, because ". . . God so loved the world that he gave his only Son" [1] to save it. The church is set apart from the world to the end that in Christ it might witness to the world. God's love for the world is what joins the church and the world to each other and calls the church to love the world, to live in it, and to serve it.

3. The church cannot consent to the world, be dominated by it, or accommodate itself to the world's standards. St. Paul gives the formula, "Don't let the world around you squeeze you into its own mould, but let God re-mould your minds from within, so that you may prove in practice that the Plan of God for you is good, meets all His demands and moves towards the goal of true maturity." [2]

4. The church cannot stand under the Cross without accepting the obligation to share with all men the redemption that was there won for it. The church is in the world, above all else, to proclaim to all men the redemption of the world by our Lord Jesus Christ, to bring to them the

means of grace, and to announce the hope of glory in the world to come.

IN HISTORY—BEYOND HISTORY

The church knows that no progress in civilization and culture can reach the goal of history that is beyond history. It knows, too, as Emil Brunner has pointed out, that "No setbacks, not even the complete destruction of civilized life, can deflect history from that ultimate goal which is beyond itself. In this sense, the Christian faith is 'other-worldly' and the Church should not be ashamed of saying so." [3]

In the unfolding process of history, civilizations and cultures come and go. They belong to this time-world. Man, too, as he appears on this temporal stage, comes and goes. But as a person—created in God's image—he is not meant to pass away. He is destined for eternity. This is why—and mark well!—the main concern of the church cannot be centered in any civilization or culture.

The church has the obligation and authority to preach an accomplished redemption because it is a redeemed community. In so doing it passes on that which it has received. It is in sharing the divine life that the church is the church and remains in the apostolic succession. St. John writes in his first letter, ". . . that which we have seen and heard we proclaim also to you, so that you may have fellowship with us; and our fellowship is with the Father and with his Son Jesus Christ." [4] And St. Paul writes in his first letter to the congregation in Corinth, "For I received from the Lord what I also delivered to you." [5] The church cannot evade the duty of passing on the inheritance in Christ Jesus without cutting itself off from the divine life in which it lives.

This is why the church witnesses to an otherworldliness that expresses itself in concern for this world, to God who is other than the world but whose world it is, a redemption that is both present and ". . . ready to be revealed in the last time." [6]

This is an hour when the Lord is forcing us to see the whole destiny of the human race in the light of his eternal purpose. The church must give attention to everything that happens because ". . . God will bring every deed into judgment." [7]

The church dare not get the eternal mislaid with the contemporary. Rather it must discern and announce God's activity in the unfolding processes of history—now! Our newspapers tell us why this or that is happening in terms of the forces of our time. The church must look at what is happening in terms of what God is doing. "Ye shall be my witnesses" [8]—let the church never forget that! We must discern the hand of God in the events of our time and then we must declare it to the world.

The deeds of God are not in the past only but in the future. "We are," as Daniel J. Niles reminds us, "witnesses of God, primarily by being part of the evidence ourselves." [9] The church is in Christ and must make this quality of being in Christ available to the world. The world may not listen. That is beside the point! The world didn't listen to Christ either. The world may ridicule or persecute. That, too, is beside the point! Christ's throne on earth became a Cross. "If the world hates you, know that it has hated me before it hated you. . . . If they persecuted me, they will persecute you." [10] On the other hand, he warned his disciples, "Woe to you, when all men speak well of you." [11]

The church must communicate with the world. Much of what we say is of little interest to the world because we address ourselves to questions the world does not ask, and our message often presumes Biblical knowledge the world of today has lost or never learned. More than that, communication is not a one-way proposition. It is a dialogue. The world has much to tell the church and the church had better listen attentively. God speaks to the world through the church. He also speaks to the church through the world.

The patterns of evangelism need to be evaluated. They make little or no impact on the masses who have no knowledge of the Christian faith. This is particularly true of the inner city, where evangelism programs and techniques are least effective in witnessing to those who have greatest influence in industry, education, government, science, the press, and other mass communications media.

A great deal more attention must be given to communicating the gospel relevantly. This means buying newspaper and magazine space, using radio and television opportunities to fullest advantage, establishing information centers, producing tracts of quality and appearance and content, providing books that present Christianity so vitally that they become best sellers in the secular book shops. Costly as all this is, it must nevertheless have high priority.

The church—acting corporately and through individual members—has to go out to men where they are in their need, pain, and bewilderment, to get under their loads and help to bear them. The church is under compulsion to do these things because they are the things that love, under the Cross, must do. The gospel is not told in love unless every effort is made to relate it to the conditions of man today.

It was that constraining love that sent a Harvard graduate lawyer to fend for the defenseless slum dwellers in Harlem; that compelled the dean of a university to resign because the rights of a Negro student had been denied; that inspired an inner city redevelopment consultant to move into the inner city in order to know the problems of the people to the end that their welfare might be protected; that effected the merger of a white congregation and a Negro congregation; that sent a retired medical doctor and his wife, a trained nurse, to Afghanistan; that led an owner of undesirable apartment houses to rehabilitate them without raising rents; that created a saving fellowship made up of Indian Americans, migrants, and people of various nationalities in a rural community; that caused a congregation in a suburb to establish a summer camp for underprivileged children; that sustains those ". . . who carry music in their heart through dusty street and crowded mart."

Now, not tomorrow, is the time to be willing to be used. God doesn't wait until we are perfect to use us. He is willing to use the imperfect instruments. What matters is that the instruments should be available for him to use. The results of our efforts are in his hands, not in ours. He tells us that we are to take no thought to the harvest but only to the proper sowing.

The door is open to those who want to do something truly creative for their loved ones, their community, their church and the world. Let such persons join the universal fellowship of intercession, thereby adding their threads of love to the fabric of the kingdom of heaven. This much at least we can all do now, and when there is more for us to do God will show us the way. We cannot really pray for people without being ready and willing to bear burdens and share fellowship.

Our membership in the Body of Christ is to be the ruling fact about us. Crossing over to the divine side with all its powers, we must take an humble place in the ranks; become part of the reasonable, holy sacrifice. It means that in work and prayer, suffering and self conquest, we are never to forget that we do not act alone or for ourselves. We act with and for the whole body. The prayer of the individual Christian is always the prayer of the whole church and therefore is infinite in its scope.

Because the church's final frontiers are beyond the ends of the earth, we must regard every station in life as an outpost to be established for Christ. Industry—trade unions —national and local government—professions—home—laboratory—school—community—farm—recreational—all provide the scene for the Christian witness. The church can never rest—its task always unfinished—until "The kingdom of the world has become the kingdom of our Lord and of his Christ, and he shall reign for ever and ever." [12]

The church knows that since the Death, Resurrection, and Ascension of Jesus Christ the world awaits the fulfillment of its purpose in history. When and how the new heaven and the new earth are to be brought to pass is not explained, but the purposes of God keep on being fulfilled in history, and their final fulfillment is undeniable fact.

The world is caught in time-panic, since time is running out. The church, however, lives in time against the backdrop of eternity. Its attitude toward the future is one of expectancy. The more expectant it is the more zealous it is in being about our Lord's business—on the edge of the edge

of history's final goal and reaching toward him who prom-
ised "I will come again and will take you to myself, that
where I am you may be also." [13]

And the prayer of the expectant church when it is true to
its mission and nature, and when it sees in faith the waiting Father, cries out:

> Master, give us life today,
> Life strong and triumphant, life full, free and eternal.
>
> Give us the fulness of physical life
> In these the swift perishing habitations of Thy Spirit.
> Give us the fulness of mental life
> In these poor tools whereby we strive to think
>   thy thoughts again.
>
> Give us the fulness of spiritual life—
> The abounding glory of Thine own indwelling,
> Whereby, in space and time, we may live the ever-
>   lasting life which is thyself.[14]

REFERENCES

CHAPTER 1.

1. Drucker, Peter F. *Landmarks of Tomorrow*, p. ix. New York: Harper and Brothers, 1959.
2. Forman, Charles W. *A Faith for the Nations*, p. 10. Philadelphia: The Westminster Press, 1957.
3. *Architectural Forum*, Sept., 1959, p. 95.
4. *Time*, June 20, 1960, p. 14.
5. Knowles, Clayton. *The New York Times*, Feb. 3, 1957.
6. Lee, Robert. *The Social Sources of Church Unity*, p. 86. Nashville: Abingdon Press, 1960.
7. Dawson, Christopher. *Religion and Culture*, p. 114. London and New York: Sheed and Ward, Ltd., 1948.
8. Marty, Martin E. *The New Shape of American Religion*, p. 74. New York: Harper and Brothers, 1959.
9. *Ibid.*
10. Folkemer, Lawrence. *Christianity and Modern Paganism*, p. 29. Philadelphia: Muhlenberg Press, 1959.
11. Heilbroner, Robert L. *The Future as History*, pp. 14-15. New York: Harper and Brothers, 1960.

CHAPTER 2.

1. Phillips, J. B. *God Our Contemporary*, p. 63. New York: The Macmillan Co., 1960.

2. *The Christian Hope and the Task of the Church:* Report of the Advisory Commission on the Main Theme of the Second Assembly, section "Christ—The Hope of the World," p. 1. New York: Harper and Brothers, 1954.

3. Eph. 3:10.

4. Heb. 7:25.

5. 2 Tim. 1:12.

6. Rom. 8:37-39.

7. John 20:21.

8. Acts 1:8.

9. Matt. 28:19.

10. 2 Cor. 5:19.

11. Matt. 28:20.

12. Heb. 12:1.

13. 2 Cor. 5:20.

14. Howe, Reuel L. *Man's Need and God's Action,* pp. 45-46. Greenwich, Conn.: Seabury Press, 1953.

15. Crotty, Horace. *The Church Victorious,* pp. 64-65. New York: Longmans Green and Co., Inc., 1938.

16. Forman, Charles W. *A Faith for the Nations,* p. 68. Philadelphia: Westminster Press, 1957.

17. Rom. 12:2.

18. Acts 15:28.

19. Wedel, Theodore O. *The Pulpit Rediscovers Theology,* pp. 129-30. Greenwich, Conn.: Seabury Press, 1956.

20. John 5:17.

21. John 9:4.

22. Heb. 11:10.

23. Adapted from "On Holy Errand," by Lloyd L. Burke in the pamphlet *Mission: Metropolis.* Private printing.

CHAPTER 3.

1. New York: Friendship Press, 1955.

2. Middleton, W. Vernon. *Methodism in Alaska and Hawaii*, p. 109. New York: Board of Missions of the Methodist Church, 1958.

3. Tunnard, Christopher, and Reed, Henry Hope. *American Skyline*, p. 248. Boston: Houghton Mifflin Co., 1955.

4. Hoiberg, Otto G. *Exploring the Small Community*, pp. 6, 7. Lincoln: University of Nebraska Press, 1955.

5. Lazareth, William H. "The Mission of the Church," in *Every Tribe and Tongue*, p. 38. New York: Friendship Press, 1960.

6. Johnson, Philip A. "Every Congregation an Intercultural Community," in *From People to People*, edited by Theodore E. Matson and Rudolph Burke. Rock Island, Ill.: Augustana Book Concern, 1960.

7. Acts 4:32.

8. Eph. 2:8-9.

CHAPTER 4.

1. Barber, Joseph. *Good Fences Make Good Neighbors*, p. 19. Indianapolis: Bobbs-Merrill Co., Inc., 1958.

2. *Maclean's Magazine*, June 15, 1951, p. 2.

3. The non-French Roman Catholics also use English, even in Quebec. It has been said that there is sharper rivalry between French Roman Catholics and Irish Roman Catholics than between Irish Roman Catholics and English Protestants.

4. Mutchmor, James R. "Don't Take Canada for Granted," in *The Christian Century*, Aug. 12, 1959, p. 918.

5. In 1867 Canada became a dominion with its own parliament.

6. Other Baptist groups, the Mennonites, and the Pentacostals have loose federations.

7. Walsh, H. H. *The Christian Church in Canada*, p. 340. Toronto: Ryerson Press, 1956.

8. Unfortunately all the member bodies of the Canadian Lu-

theran Council have their denominational loyalties in the U.S.A. There are indications that in the near future all of them will be indigenous to Canada.

CHAPTER 5.

1. Kloetzli, Walter, and Hillman, Arthur. *Urban Church Planning*, p. 1. Philadelphia: Muhlenberg Press, 1958.

2. Allen, Roland. *Missionary Methods: St. Paul's or Ours*, pp. 19-23. Chicago: Moody Press, 1959.

3. The author has watched the development of the Roman Catholic rural church program for the past ten years, particularly in Minnesota, North and South Dakota. The headquarters of the Catholic Rural Life program is Fargo, North Dakota, a strong Lutheran state.

4. 2 Cor. 8:14.

5. 1 Cor. 12:26.

6. A judicatory is an administrative unit of a denomination, on the regional, state, or county level.

7. Bouquet, A. C. *The Christian Faith and Non-Christian Religions*, p. 206. Digswell Place, England: James Nisbet and Co., Ltd., 1958. (U. S. publisher: Harper and Brothers.)

8. *Christ for the Moving Millions*, pp. 43-44. Chicago: Division of American Missions, National Lutheran Council, 1955.

9. Ruoss, Meryl. "The Churches and Urban Redevelopment (a panel discussion)," in *The City Church*, May-June, 1957.

10. See *The Christian Century*, June 10, 1959, pp. 698-701.

11. In a statement made at a meeting of the Division of American Missions, National Lutheran Council, 1957.

12. "Your Minister: His Job, His Problems," in *Changing Times*, Nov., 1959, p. 25.

13. Neill, Stephen. *The Unfinished Task*, p. 66-67. London: Edinburgh House Press, 1957.

14. Luke 10:2.

CHAPTER 6.

1. 1 Cor. 1:12-13.
2. *Ibid.*, 3:9.
3. Phillips, J. B. *Letters to Young Churches: A Translation of the New Testament Epistles*, p. 109. New York: The Macmillan Co., 1952.
4. 1 Cor. 12:27.
5. Eph. 2:10.
6. Lange, John D. "The Churches and Urban Redevelopment (a panel discussion)," in *The City Church*, May-June, 1957.
7. Ross, D. Reid. "Churches and Public Agencies—why, how can they team up for housing renewal?" in *Journal of Housing*, June, 1959, p. 192.
8. Kloetzli, Walter. "Churchmen Have Important Role to Play in Urban Renewal," in *Journal of Housing*, July, 1956, p. 244.
9. A mimeographed report. New York: Division of Home Missions, National Council of Churches, Feb. 4, 1957.
10. Hoyer, H. Conrad. *Concerning "Planning Together with Other Protestants."* A mimeographed report prepared for the Division of American Missions of the National Lutheran Council, Feb. 4, 1959.

CHAPTER 7.

1. 2 Cor. 4:10.
2. 1 Cor. 12:27.
3. Acts 2:42.
4. Acts 2:44.
5. Acts 2:47.
6. John 10:29.
7. John 10:16.
8. Heb. 10:25.

9. Ps. 122:1.
10. Luke 18:13.
11. Kean, Charles Duell. *The Christian Gospel and the Parish Church*, pp. 136-37. Greenwich, Conn.: Seabury Press, 1953.
12. Bergendoff, Conrad. *I Believe in the Church*, pp. 49-50. Rock Island, Ill.: Augustana Book Concern, 1937.
13. Southcott, Ernest W. *The Parish Comes Alive*, p. 1. New York: Morehouse-Gorham Co., 1956.
14. James 1:23-24.
15. Southcott, *op. cit.*, p. 140.

CHAPTER 8.

1. John 3:8.
2. Cowper, William. "Light Shining Out of Darkness," in *Olney Hymns*, 1779.
3. Bonhoeffer, Dietrich. *Life Together*, p. 29. New York: Harper and Brothers, 1954.

CHAPTER 9.

1. 1 Pet. 2:5.
2. 1 Pet. 2:9.
3. John 8:12.
4. Matt. 5:14.
5. John 14:12.
6. John 20:21.
7. Matt. 28:19.
8. John 15:5.
9. Matt. 28:20.
10. *The Christian Hope and the Task of the Church*, section "The Laity: The Christian in His Vocation," p. 1. New York: Harper and Brothers, 1954.
11. 1 Cor. 3:21-23.
12. Eph. 4:11.

13. Webber, George W. *God's Colony in Man's World*, p. 129. Nashville: Abingdon Press, 1960.
14. Heiges, Donald R. *The Christian's Calling*, p. 102. Philadelphia: Muhlenberg Press, 1958.
15. 1 Cor. 9:22.
16. Kean, Charles Duell. *The Christian Gospel and the Parish Church*, pp. 133-34. Greenwich, Conn.: Seabury Press, 1953.
17. John 15:16.
18. Ps. 66:4.
19. Rom. 12:1.

CHAPTER 10.

1. John 3:16.
2. Phillips, J. B. *Letters to Young Churches: A Translation of the New Testament Epistles*, p. 28. New York: The Macmillan Co., 1952.
3. Brunner, Emil. *Christianity and Civilization*, p. 141. New York: Charles Scribner's Sons, 1949.
4. 1 John 1:3.
5. 1 Cor. 11:23.
6. 1 Pet. 1:5.
7. Eccl. 12:14.
8. Acts 1:8.
9. *The Pulpit*, Aug., 1960. Published by *The Christian Century*.
10. John 15:18, 20.
11. Luke 6:26.
12. Rev. 11:15.
13. John 14:3.
14. Hoyland, John S. *A Book of Prayers Written for Use in an Indian College*, p. 84. London: The Challenge Limited.

READING LIST

Leaders of study groups may order the Friendship Press books listed below from denominational literature headquarters. From these same sources, they may also order *Adult Guide on "Churches for New Times,"* by Richard Brown, priced at 75 cents, which contains program plans for using *Edge of the Edge* and other Friendship Press materials.

Books of other publishers are listed as additional resources. They may be found in bookstores and libraries.

FRIENDSHIP PRESS BOOKS, 1961

Foster, Virgil E. *By Deed and Design.* Stories of churches that have met creatively the challenge of new times. Cloth, $2.95; paper $1.95.

Everett, Harvey A. *The Future Won't Wait.* Presents the opportunities for young people in our changing church and community situations. Cloth, $2.95; paper, $1.75.

BOOKS OF OTHER PUBLISHERS

Allen, Roland. *Missionary Methods: St. Paul's or Ours.* Chicago: Moody Press, 1959.

Bergendoff, Conrad. *The One Holy Catholic Apostolic Church.* Rock Island, Ill.: Augustana Book Concern, 1954.

Berry, Ruth Murhead. *High Is the Wall*. Philadelphia: Muhlenberg Press, 1960.

Bonhoeffer, Dietrich. *Life Together*. New York: Harper and Brothers, 1954.

Brown, Robert McAfee. *The Significance of the Church*. Philadelphia: Westminster Press, 1956.

Brunner, Emil. *Christianity and Civilization*. New York: Charles Scribner's Sons, 1949.

Carlson, Edgar M. *The Church and the Public Conscience*. Philadelphia: Muhlenberg Press, 1956.

Christ for the Moving Millions. (Papers presented at a Conference on Mobility in 1954.) Chicago: Division of American Missions, National Lutheran Council, 1955.

Clifford, Paul Rowntree. *The Mission of the Local Church*. London: Student Christian Movement Press, Ltd., 1953.

Dietrich, Suzanne de. *The Witnessing Community*. Philadelphia: The Westminster Press, 1958.

Dilemmas and Opportunities. (Report of a Study Conference on Christian Action in Rapid Social Change.) New York: Department on Church and Society, Division of Studies, World Council of Churches, 1959.

Drucker, Peter F. *Landmarks of Tomorrow*. New York: Harper and Brothers, 1959.

Eckardt, A. Roy. *The Surge of Piety in America*. New York: Association Press, 1958.

Emrich, Richard S. *Earth Might Be Fair*. New York: Harper and Brothers, New York, 1945.

Folkemer, Lawrence D. *Christianity and Modern Paganism*. Philadelphia: Muhlenberg Press, 1959.

Forman, Charles W. *A Faith for the Nations*. Philadelphia: Westminster Press, 1957.

Fortune, The Editors of. *Markets of the Sixties*. New York: Harper and Brothers, 1960.

————. *The Exploding Metropolis*. Garden City, N. Y.: Double-day and Co., 1958.

Greene, Shirley E. *Ferment on the Fringe*. Philadelphia: Christian Education Press, 1960.

Handlin, Oscar. *Race and Nationality in American Life*. (An Anchor Book.) New York: Doubleday and Co., 1957.

Haseldon, Kyle. *The Racial Problem in Christian Perspective*. New York: Harper and Brothers, 1959.

Heiges, Donald R. *The Christian's Calling*. Philadelphia: Muhlenberg Press, 1958.

Heilbroner, Robert L. *The Future as History*. New York: Harper and Brothers, 1960.

Heinecken, Martin J. *God In the Space Age*. Philadelphia: John C. Winston Co., 1959.

Hoiberg, Otto G. *Exploring the Small Community*. Lincoln: University of Nebraska Press, 1955.

Jenkins, Daniel. *The Strangeness of the Church*. New York: Doubleday and Co., 1955.

Kantonen, T. A. *Resurgence of the Gospel*. Philadelphia: Muhlenberg Press, 1948.

Kean, Charles Duell. *The Christian Gospel and the Parish Church*. Greenwich, Conn.: Seabury Press, 1953.

Kloetzli, Walter, and Hillman, Arthur. *Urban Church Planning*. Philadelphia: Muhlenberg Press, 1958.

Kraemer, Hendrik. *A Theology of the Laity*. Philadelphia: Westminster Press, 1959.

Lee, Robert. *The Social Sources of Church Unity*. Nashville: Abingdon Press, 1960.

Letts, Harold C. *Christian Social Responsibility*. Three volumes. Philadelphia: Muhlenberg Press, 1957.

Loew, Cornelius. *Modern Rivals to Christian Faith*. Philadelphia: Westminster Press, 1956.

Marty, Martin E. *The New Shape of American Religion.* New York: Harper and Brothers, 1959.

Maus, Cynthia Pearl. *Christ and the Fine Arts.* New York: Harper and Brothers, 1960.

Miller, Donald G. *The Nature and Mission of the Church.* Richmond: John Knox Press, 1957.

Neill, Stephen. *The Unfinished Task.* London: Lutterworth Press, 1957. Distributed by Friendship Press. $3.00.

Niebuhr, H. Richard. *The Purpose of the Church and Its Ministry.* New York: Harper and Brothers, 1956.

Pelikan, Jaroslav. *The Riddle of Roman Catholicism.* Nashville: Abingdon Press, 1959.

Rodenmayer, Robert N. *We Have This Ministry.* New York: Harper and Brothers, 1959.

Rowland, Stanley J. *Land in Search of God.* New York: Random House, 1958.

Southcott, Ernest W. *The Parish Comes Alive.* New York: Morehouse-Gorham Co., 1956.

Tomkins, Oliver. *The Wholeness of the Church.* London: Student Christian Movement Press, 1949.

Walker, Alan. *The Whole Gospel for the Whole Church.* Nashville: Abingdon Press, 1957.

Walsh, H. H. *The Christian Church in Canada.* Toronto: Ryerson Press, 1956.

Weatherford, W. D. *American Churches and the Negro.* Boston: Christopher Publishing House, 1957.

Webber, George W. *God's Colony in Man's World.* Nashville: Abingdon Press, 1960.

A WORD ABOUT THE FORMAT . . .

This book was set in Janson, 10 point leaded 3 points.
Anton Janson's type faces were first shown in Leipsic,
Germany, about 1675. Although Janson is known as a
Dutch type face, Wolffgang Erhardt is presumed to have
bought the original matrices from the Edling heirs
(Edling was Janson's successor in Germany) then liv-
ing in Holland.

MANUFACTURED BY *Book Craftsmen Associates, Inc., New York*
JACKETS AND PAPER COVERS BY *Affiliated Lithographers, Inc.,
    New York*
TEXT PAPER: *S. D. Warren's #66 Antique*
TYPOGRAPHIC DESIGN BY *Barbara M. Knox*
BINDING BY *Louise E. Jefferson*